Teresa Franceschini
Staten Island, N.Y.

1

MONASTERY
Prayer, Work, Community

M. Basil Pennington, O.C.S.O.
Photographs by Nicolas Sapieha

1817

A Scala Book, Published by Harper & Row, Publishers, San Francisco

Cambridge, Hagerstown, New York, Philadelphia, London, Mexico City, São Paulo, Sydney

Produced by Scala, Florence, Italy
Project directed by Maria Teresa Train
Designed by Lavinia Branca and Catherine Hopkins
Printed in Italy

FIRST EDITION

Library of Congress Cataloging in Publication Data

Pennington, M. Basil.
    Monastery : prayer, work, and community.

    "A Scala book."
    Bibliography: p.
    1. Monastic and religious life.   2. Monasticism and religious
orders.   I. Sapieha, Nicolas.   II. Title.
BX2435.P443   1983   255   83—47732
ISBN 0—06—066495—9

Contents

Prologue: Thomas Merton on the Monastic Life   13

1. A Living Tradition 29

2. *Ora, Labora, Vita Communis*—Prayer, Work, Community 53

3. In Our Time 89

   Chronology of Monasticism 105

   For Further Reading 115

   Color Plate Captions 121

Matins

When the full fields begin to smell of sunrise
And the valleys sing in their sleep,
The pilgrim moon pours over the solemn darkness
Her waterfalls of silence,
And then departs, up the long avenue of trees.

The stars hide, in the glade, their light, like tears,
And tremble where some train runs, lost,
Baying in eastward mysteries of distance,
Where fire flares, somewhere, over a sink of cities.

Now kindle in the windows of this ladyhouse, my soul,
Your childish, clear awakeness:
Burn in the country night
Your wise and sleepless lamp.
For, from the frowning tower, the windy belfry,
Sudden the bells come, bridegrooms,
And fill the echoing dark with love and fear.

—Thomas Merton

On the Monastic Life

Let us suppose the message of a so-called contemplative to a so-called man of the world to be something like this:

My dear Brother, first of all, I apologize for addressing you when you have not addressed me and have not really asked me anything. And I apologize for being behind a high wall which you do not understand. This high wall is to you a problem, and perhaps it is also a problem to me. Perhaps you ask me why I stay behind it out of obedience? Perhaps you are no longer satisfied with the reply that if I stay behind this wall I have quiet, recollection, tranquility of heart. It is true that when I came to this monastery where I am, I came in revolt against the meaningless confusion of a life in which there was so much activity, so much movement, so much useless talk, so much superficial and needless stimulation, that I could not remember who I was. But the fact remains that my flight from the world is not a reproach to you who remain in the world, and I have no right to repudiate the world in a purely negative fashion, because if I do that my flight will have taken me not to truth and to God but to a private, though doubtless pious, illusion.

Can I tell you that I have found answers to the questions that torment the man of our time? I do not know if I have found answers. When I first became a monk, yes, I was more sure of 'answers.' But as I grow old in the monastic life and advance further into solitude, I become aware that I have only begun to seek the questions. And what are the questions? Can man make sense out of his existence? Can man honestly give his life meaning merely by adopting a certain set of explanations which pretend to tell him why the world began and where it will end, why there is evil and what is necessary for a good life? My brother, perhaps in my solitude I have become as it were an explorer for you, a searcher in realms which you are not able to visit. I have been summoned to explore a desert area of man's heart in which explanations no longer suffice, and in which one learns that only experience counts. An arid, rocky, dark land of the soul, sometimes illuminated by strange fires which men fear and peopled by spectres which men studiously avoid except in their nightmares. And in this area I have learned that one cannot truly know hope unless he has found out how like despair hope is. The language of Christianity has said this for centuries in other less naked terms. But the language of Christianity has been so used and so misused that sometimes you distrust it: you do not know whether or not behind the word 'cross' there stands the experience of mercy and salvation, or only the threat of punishment. If my word means anything to you, I can say to you that I have experienced the cross to mean mercy and not cruelty, truth and not deception; that the news of the truth and love of Jesus is indeed the true good news, but in our time it speaks out in strange places. And perhaps it speaks out in you more than it does in me; perhaps Christ is nearer to you than he is to me. This I say without shame or guilt because I have learned to rejoice that Jesus is in the world in people who know Him not, that He is at work in them when they think themselves far from Him, and it is my joy to tell you to hope though you think that for you of all men hope is impossible. Hope not because you think you can be good, but because God loves us irrespective of our merits and whatever is good in us comes from His love, not from our own doing. Hope because Jesus is with those who are poor and outcast and perhaps despised even by those who should seek them and care for them more lovingly because they act in God's name.

God is not a 'problem' and we who live the contemplative life have learned by experience that one cannot know God as long as one seeks to solve 'the problem of God'. To seek to solve the problem of God is to seek to see one's own eyes. One cannot see one's own eyes because they are that with which one sees and God is the light by which we see—by which we see not a clearly defined 'object' called God, but everything else in the invisible One. God is then the Seer and the Seeing and the Seen. God seeks Himself in us, and the aridity and sorrow of our heart is the sorrow of God who is not known to us, who cannot yet find Himself in us because we do not dare to believe or trust the incredible truth that He could live in us, and live there out of choice, out of preference. But indeed we exist solely for this, to be the place He has chosen for His presence, His manifestation in the world, His epiphany. But we make all this dark and inglorious because we fail to believe it, we refuse to believe it. It is not that we hate God, rather that we hate ourselves, despair of ourselves. If we once began to recognize, humbly but truly, the real value of our own self, we would see that this value was the sign of God in our being, the signature of God upon our being.

The contemplative is not the man who has fiery visions of the cherubim carrying God on their imagined chariot, but simply he who has risked his mind in the desert beyond language and beyond ideas where God is encountered in the nakedness of pure trust, that is to say in the surrender of our own poverty and incompleteness in order no longer to clench our minds in a cramp upon themselves, as if thinking made us exist. The message of hope the contemplative offers you, then, is not that you need to find your way through the jungle of language and problems that today surround God; but that whether you understand or not, God loves you, is present to you, lives in you, dwells in you, calls you, saves you, and offers you an understanding and light which are like nothing you ever found in books or heard in sermons. The contemplative has nothing to tell you except to reassure you and say that if you dare to penetrate your own silence and dare to advance without fear into the solitude of your own heart, and risk sharing that solitude with the lonely other who seeks God through you and with you, then you will truly recover the light and the capacity to understand what is beyond words and beyond explanations because it is too close to be explained: it is the intimate union in the depths of your own heart, of God's spirit and your own secret inmost self, so that you and He are in all truth One Spirit. I love you, in Christ.

—Thomas Merton

This passage is from a hastily written letter addressed to the Abbot of the Cistercian monastery of Fratrocchie near Rome in response to a request of Pope Paul VI for "a message of contemplatives to the world." The letter was written in 1967, the year before Merton died.

After the Night Office

It is not yet the grey and frosty time
When barns ride out of the night like ships:
We do not see the Brothers, bearing lanterns,
Sink in the quiet mist,
As various as the spirits who, with lamps, are sent
To search our souls' Jerusalems
Until our houses are at rest
And minds enfold the Word, our Guest.

Praises and canticles anticipate
Each day the singing bells that wake the sun,
But now our psalmody is done.
Our hasting souls outstrip the day:
Now, before dawn, they have their noon.
The Truth that transsubstantiates the body's night
Has made our minds His temple-tent:
Open the secret eye of faith
And drink these deeps of invisible light.

The weak walls
Of the world fall
And heaven, in floods, comes pouring in:
Sink from your shallows, soul, into eternity,
And slake your wonder at that deep-lake spring.
We touch the rays we cannot see,
We feel the light that seems to sing.

—Thomas Merton

PRAYER

The entire life of a monk or nun is geared toward fostering an interior life that opens out upon the whole of the creation and the entire human family in a magnificent embrace of love.

1.

A Living Tradition

> While still living in the palace, Abba Arsenius prayed to God in these words, "Lord,
> lead me in the way of salvation." And a voice came saying to him, "Arsenius, flee
> from men and you will be saved."
> Having withdrawn to the solitary life, he made the same prayer again and he heard a
> voice saying to him, "Arsenius, flee, be silent, pray always, for these are the source of
> sinlessness."

The Arsenius in question was the tutor of the Princes Arcadius and Honorius, sons of Theodosius I. The place was the imperial palace at Byzantium. The year was A.D. 394. Arsenius went to Scetis in Egypt and placed himself under the tutelage of Abba John the Dwarf.

When Arsenius fled into the desert to pursue a way of salvation, he was certainly not the first. Indeed, many centuries before Christ, his Master, walked the earth, men and women were pursuing the monastic way of life in the remote vastness of the Himalayas, in the caves of Arunachala, and in many other places. At the edge of almost every great religion—the inner edge rather than the outer—there have been monastics. Geographical apartness, however relative it might be, is of the essence of monastic life, an apartness for which the monk and nun have always had to struggle. The world wants to keep its own. Arsenius had to flee from the court secretly. The world has ever pursued the monk. Even the great Saint Anthony had to move repeatedly, ever more deeply into the desert, and in the end he had to relinquish his hideaway and serve those who came in pursuit of him.

If the world no longer comes clamoring after the monk, he must still struggle with the world he brings with him into solitude, the worldliness within his own heart. In this struggle, monks have perhaps been even less successful. This worldliness still lurking in the recesses of a monk's heart continues to be seductive. It tries to fill his solitude with its pleasure and cares or impel him to go out from his solitude to involve himself in many activities. Saint John Cassian defined the scope of the monastic life as this: to attain purity of heart and to empty the heart of all earthly attachments so that it can be free, be silent, hear God, and pray always.

Christians have ample witness from their divine Master of the importance of going apart, at least periodically. He initiated his ministry with forty days in the wilderness. In the midst of his busy public career, with all its pressing demands, he repeatedly withdrew into the mountains or some other solitary place to be alone with his Father to open his heart in prayer.

In the first years after Christ's ascension, the choice to follow the way of Jesus was enough to set one apart. Persecutions increased that apartness. Prison, exile, and death were apt to be the lot of a despised and hunted people. But within a couple of centuries Christianity conquered, and in the conquest it was itself conquered. In overcoming the so-called civilized world and the masters of that world, it became worldly. It was then that courtiers like Arsenius heard the voice: "Flee."

When Arsenius arrived in Scetis he found that many had gotten there before him; the deserts of Egypt were well populated by monks and nuns. Abba Anthony—often called Anthony the Great, the Father of monks—was born in Central Egypt in A.D. 251. When he was eighteen he heard the Lord speak to him through the proclamation of the Gospel during the Liturgy: "Go, sell all that you have and give to the poor and come. . . ." In response, he divested himself and took up a simple, ascetical life on the outskirts of his village under the guidance of a recluse. There always were in the Christian community those who chose the "better part" of Mary while the Marthas were busy about many things.

Sixteen years later Anthony withdrew into the desert, seeking greater solitude. His reputation grew, and as the persecutions drew to a close, disciples pursued him. In A.D. 310 he retired into even greater solitude, though his solitude was never a withdrawal from the Church. Twice before he died at the age of 105 he journeyed to Alexandria; once to be with the martyrs in a time of persecution, and again to support the bishop, Saint Athanasius, in his sufferings at the hands of heretics. Athanasius thus came to know the saint first hand; and through his biography of the Great Anthony, not only the saint, but the monastic way of life became known throughout the empire.

The period of the fourth and fifth centuries had many similarities to our own. There was an unprecedented unity and communication among peoples. Athanasius, for example, was repeatedly sent into exile from Africa to various parts of Europe and Asia. The increasing affluence of the few weighed ever more heavily on enslaved peoples and nations. More and more young (and not so young) men and women decided that a system based on materialistic progress was not worth the investment of their lives. They left the lecture halls of Rome and Athens, government positions and successful enterprises, prosperous families and great estates, and headed east in search of true wisdom. In Syria, Palestine, Arabia, and the deserts of Egypt, they sought a spiritual father or mother and asked for a "word of life."

A brother asked Abba Ammonas, "Give me a word," and the old man replied, "Go make your thoughts like those of the evildoers who are in the prison. For they are always asking when the magistrate will come, awaiting him in anxiety. Even so the monk ought to give himself at all times to accusing his own soul, saying, 'Unhappy wretch that I am. How shall I stand before the judgment seat of Christ? What shall I say to him in my defense?' If you give yourself continually to this, you may be saved."

Someone asked Abba Anthony, "What must I do in order to please God?" The old man replied, "Pay attention to what I tell you: whoever you may be, always have God before your eyes; whatever you do, do it according to the testimony of the Scriptures; in whatever place you live, do not easily leave it. Keep these three precepts and you will be saved."

Abba Pambo asked Abba Anthony, "What ought I to do?" and the old man said to him, "Do not trust in your own righteousness, do not worry about the past, but control your tongue and your stomach."

A man asked Abba Benjamin, "Give me a word." The old man said, "If you observe the following you can be saved: Be joyful at all times, pray without ceasing, and give thanks for all things."

A brother questioned Abba Herman, saying, "Give me a word. How can I be saved?" The old man said to him, "Sit in your cell, and if you are hungry, eat; if you are thirsty, drink; only do not speak evil of anyone, and you will be saved."

Abba Joseph asked Abba Or, "Give me a word." And he said to him, "Do you trust me?" He replied that he did. Then he said to him, "What you have seen me do, do also."

They lived with them and followed their example:

Abba Stephen said, "When I was younger, I lived with Abba Gelasios. He did not tell me to do anything, but he himself set the table and said to me: 'Brother, if you want to, come and eat.' I replied, 'I have come to learn, why do you never tell me to do anything?' But the old man gave me no reply whatever. So I went to tell the seniors. They came and said to him, 'Abba, the brother has come to your holiness in order to learn. Why do you never tell him to do anything?' The old man said to them, 'Am I an *abba*, that I should give orders? As far as I am concerned, I do not tell him anything, but if he wishes he can do what he sees me doing.' From that moment I took the initiative and did what the old man did. As for him, he did what he did in silence, so he taught me in silence."

When Abba Daniel lived in the desert he was beset by weariness and attacked by many sinful thoughts. He said to God, "Lord, I want to be saved, but these thoughts do not leave me alone; what shall I do in my affliction? How can I be saved?" A short while afterwards, when he got up to go out, Daniel saw a man like himself sitting at his work, getting up from his work to pray, then sitting down and plaiting a basket, then getting up to pray again. He heard an angel say to him, "Do this and you will be saved." At these words, Daniel was filled with joy and courage. He did this, and he was saved.

They formed communities of like-minded disciples.

By God's providential design, three men came to Pachomius, and said to him, "We want to become monks in your company and serve Christ." He talked with them to know whether they would be able to renounce their parents and follow the Savior. Then he put them to the test and, having found they had the right intentions, he clothed them in the monks' habit and received them as his companions with joy and God's love.

The renown of his piety went out over all the land of Egypt. In a certain place were five brothers leading the anchoritic life: they were men valiant in the work of God. Their names were: Abba Pecos, Abba Cornelios, Abba Paul, Abba Pachomius, and Abba John. Having learned about his sound faith, they set out and came to live with him, and he accepted them, rejoicing in the Spirit. Still fifty others, who lived up river in a place called Thbakat and had likewise heard of him, came to him. He accepted them likewise, but discovering they had a carnal mind, he expelled them from his dwelling. After that, the Lord was at work in many others who came to him, and he accepted them, building them up in the law of the Lord.—*The Bohairic Life of Pachomius*

Besides the hermits—those who were led by the Holy Spirit or sometimes other spirits to live completely on their own—the monks and nuns formed two different kinds of communities. There were those who gathered around an *abba;* their coming together was wholly because of him. They were like so many spokes centered on a hub. Their relation with each other was almost accidental. These semi-eremitical communities flourished in the deserts of Egypt, at Scetis and the Cells, and elsewhere. John Cassian brought their spirit to the West in his marvelous *Conferences* and *Institutes.* At the same time other Fathers stressed much more the communal life. They could see themselves in some way the continuation of the Church of the Acts:

The whole group of believers was united, heart and soul; no one claimed for his own use anything that he had, as everything they owned was held in common. The faithful all lived together and owned everything in common; they sold their goods and possessions and shared out the proceeds among themselves according to what each one needed. They went as a body to the Temple every day but met in their homes for the breaking of bread; they shared their food gladly and generously; they praised God and were looked up to by everyone. Day by day God added to their community those destined to be saved.

Saint Pachomius was guided by angelic inspiration to form a community in this way in Egypt. Similar communities developed in Palestine. After a tour of these outposts, Basil of Cesarea, later called the Great, founded such a community in Pontus in Asia Minor. He had little esteem for the eremitical life: "If a man lives alone, whose feet is he going to wash?" And he had considerable concern for the spiritual and corporal works of mercy. The community came together as the Body of Christ; the superior served it as an eye. This tradition, too, came to Europe as Greek monks settled in Italy. Indeed, in the easy flow of the times, they would find their way even to Britain.

Benedict of Nursia gathered together these differing currents: the community centered on the *abba* and the body engendering an eye, and added to them the fraternity of the clerical community gathered around the Bishop of Hippo. It is the richness of his synthesis that makes his *Rule for Monasteries* so adaptable.

As the great Father and Founder passed on, the disciples looked more and more to literary expressions of their heritage. The *Apothegmata,* or *Sayings of the Fathers,* became fundamental sources. The monastic prescriptions of the first abbots of Pachomian monasteries were gathered together in what is called the *Rule of Pachomius.* Saint Basil's catechesis, the *Long* and *Short Rules* (ca. 372), became a guiding norm in the East and flowed into the Western tradition, especially through Saint Benedict's *Rule* (ca. 525). More directly influenced by the spirit of Roman jurisprudence, western Fathers, one after the other, wrote their rules: Alypius' *Ordo Monasterii* (ca. 395); Augustine's *Praeceptum* for the monks of Hippo (ca. 398) and *Obiurgatio* for his sister's convent (ca. 423); Caesarius of Arles' *Rule for Monks* (ca. 500) and *Rule for Virgins* (ca. 534); the *Rule of the Four Fathers,* the *Second Rule of the Fathers,* and the *Third Rule of the Fathers* (the dating and origin of these are disputed; Neufville makes them early fifth-century Italian); and the *Rule* of the unknown "Master," all leading up to the masterly *Rule for Monasteries* of Benedict of Nursia, the acclaimed "Father of Western Monasticism."

Benedict knew the tradition well. He knew of *sarabaites,* monks "still loyal to the world by their actions. They lie to God by their tonsure. Two or three together, or even alone, without a shepherd, they pen themselves up in their own sheepfolds, not the Lord's. Their law is what they like to do, whatever strikes their fancy. Anything they believe in and choose, they call holy; anything they dislike, they consider forbidden." Against such as these he prescribed a promise of obedience. He knew *gyrovagues* "who spend their entire lives drifting from region to region, staying as guests for three or four days in different monasteries. Always on the move, they never settle down, and are slaves to their own wills and gross appetites." Against these he prescribed a promise of stability. He was cautious about *anchorites* or *hermits*. They must "come through the test of living in a monastery for a long time." For this he prescribed a promise of fidelity to the monastic way of life which calls for constant conversion. Benedict was enthusiastic about *cenobites,* "those who belong to a monastery where they serve under a rule and an abbot." These were the "strongest kind," for whom he wrote his *Rule.*

As we have said already, Benedict blended the various emphases of the monastic tradition. In his monastery there is an *abba.* He himself speaks in his *Rule* as a master. The *abba* is to teach, to hold the place of Christ, but also to listen: "Nothing is to be done without consultation." The monks are to obey the abbot, and they are also to obey each other. A bit of Roman militarism creeps into his *Rule* both in its spirit and terminology. Everything is well ordered. It is a school of the Lord's service. The Work of God, standing in rank before him, singing his praises, has a paramount place: "Nothing is to be preferred to the Work of God." Twelve of the seventy-two chapters are devoted to it. There is an extensive disciplinary code which only at the end of the *Rule* blossoms into a communion of love and respect. Duties are clearly defined, members are put in their place, and so is everything else. But in the end it is a way of humility, a ladder that leads up to "that perfect love of God which casts out fear . . . love for Christ, good habit, and delight in virtue." Benedict, giving his own example of the humble monk, describes his *Rule* as a "little rule written for beginners," putting them on the path so that they "can set out for the loftier summits of teaching and virtues" pointed to by the integral monastic tradition.

This moderate *Rule,* which ordained all things so that "the strong would have something to strive after and the weak would not be driven away," coexisted for a time with many other western rules. As it moved up through Europe, it commingled with the current flowing down from Ireland where the austerities of the desert were codified with Celtic rigor.

Reformers like Saint Romuald (ca. 950–1027) insisted on the declarations of Saint Benedict's last chapter and drew on earlier traditions to orient monastic life institutionally toward a more eremitic existence. Other reforms, such as that of Cluny, would emphasize the prominence given the Work of God and expand it till it left little time for the *lectio* necessary to nourish it and the labor necessary to support life and keep it in balance. The influence of the *Rule* came to its fullest flowering in the Cistercian reform, a reform aimed at living the *Rule* to the full:

These monks had often felt grieved when they saw that no one among them kept the *Rule* of Saint Benedict with fidelity as they had taken a solemn vow to observe it. Such was the motive that brought them into a solitary place after having recourse to the Apostolic Legate. Henceforth, they could embrace the *Rule* with love and observe it in all its points, remaining faithful to their profession.   —*Exordium parvum*

The Cistercians worked for the goal that Benedict had set: "We shall run on the path of God's commandments, our hearts overflowing with the inexpressible delight of love." Thus the *Rule* became for the Cistercians a "school of love." There quickly flowered among them some of the greatest mystical writers of the Western monastic tradition: Bernard of Clairvaux, William of Saint Thierry, Isaac of Stella, Lutgard, and Mechtilde. These writers centered everything on love and were practical contemplatives who rooted mystical love in everyday monastic life. Monastic life was to be a contemplative life. And precisely as such—through the great contemplative spirits it produced—it had an immense social, economic, and even political impact on society. Paradoxically, however, the more monks attended to social, economic, and political affairs to the detriment of their contemplative life, the more their impact diminished.

The cultural and literary contributions of monks in the West, especially those of the Celtic and Benedictine traditions, cannot be minimized. But here again, it was the holiest and most contemplative men, like Bede the Venerable, who made the most outstanding contribution. Let us look a little more deeply at the inner dynamism of the monastic life.

WORK

"Then are they truly monks, when they live by the labor of their hands as did our fathers and apostles."—*Rule* of St. Benedict

42

2.

Ora, Labora, Vita Communis

Ora, labora, vita communis—prayer, work, community—these three sum up well the monastic experience.

Ora

If you ask someone what a nun or monk does, the spontaneous response will probably be: She prays. He prays. When the Great Arsenius turned to the Lord for direction, the response he received was simple and clear: "Flee, be silent, *pray always.*" The monk goes apart to find silence. In his solitude, he embraces an ascetic life to silence the clamorings within him. He seeks this silence so that he can pray, so that he can hear God and respond to him.

One day Abba Arsenius came to a place where there were reeds blowing in the wind. The old man said to the brothers, "What is this movement?" They said, "Some reeds." Then the old man said to them, "When one who is living in silent prayer hears the song of a little sparrow, his heart no longer experiences the same peace. How much worse it is when you hear the movement of those reeds."

When Father Louis (Thomas Merton) used to inveigh against the noise of the tractors and power mowers around Gethsemani Abbey, some of his brethren would smile at him good-humoredly. But this sensitive man was responding to the situation from the depths of monastic tradition.

A man or a woman goes apart to embrace the monastic life because he or she wants to find the freedom and the support to enter into a very complete union with God. By God's grace they have somehow come to see that this is what they are made for. They may or may not immediately perceive the fact that it is by such a union with God that they can make the greatest contribution to the well-being of all, that they can be most fully an instrument of God's creative and redeeming love, the source of all good.

Saint Benedict's *Rule for Monasteries* says that when a man comes to the monastery he is not to be given easy entrance. In the first days of Christian monasticism, the seeker had to make a long journey to the East. He or she had, indeed, to leave behind the comforts and values of the world. Submission to a spiritual father or mother was immediate and direct. When more established monasteries began to be found near at hand, it was feared that candidates might not be such radical seekers, that they might even be inspired by less worthy motives. In a chaotic society, the peace and security of the cloister had their natural attraction. Saint Benedict would leave the man knocking at the door four or five days and even subject him to harsh treatment before he would allow him to enter.

Today, it is rare to wait only four or five days. Vocation fathers or mothers may not be harsh, but they are demanding. Candidates will be expected to complete their secular education (whatever that might mean: some want only secondary education, others need college or even postgraduate studies to feel complete—it is a question of discernment) and to have some successful life experience. They should enter the monastery from a position of strength, in freedom, knowing they can make it in the world, that they have real options; if things don't work out in the monastery, they can freely leave and establish themselves outside. Furthermore, they will be expected to undergo physical, dental, and psychological examinations. Certainly, they will not be allowed "an easy entry."

Inside the gate, probation is not over. Benedict had his candidates spend a few days in the guest house. Today there is a period of postulancy, a continual asking, while candidates get a better look at the life and the monks or nuns get a better look at them. Then comes the novitiate. The novice master or mistress must discern if the candidates "truly seek God"—if they truly want a deep union and communion with God, a life of prayer. Saint Benedict gives the master three concrete criteria to use in this discernment: does the novice show an eagerness for a humble way of life, for obedience, and for the *Opus Dei,* the Work of God. There is an interrelation here. Only if one leaves aside ambition—the quest for status, position, and power—can one be free to seek the will of another, to seek to walk in the way of obedience. A person seeks a humble way of life in order to be free to obey—to obey to live a divine life, a life wholly in harmony with the divine, with the will of God. No human person can rate the obedience of another human person; all are equals. A person obeys others in order to be practiced in obedience so that he can completely obey God. One obeys others because God does express his will through others. The aim is to be wholly in harmony with the will of God, the movement of God. Herein lies holiness, union, and essential prayer.

The whole of creation, all its being and activity, is the opus of God, his masterpiece. Its meaning lies in his glory. All is made to glorify God. The rest of creation can adequately glorify God only if it is lifted up to him through and by the mind and heart of the human person. For the human person alone is made in the full image of God, with a mind to know him and a heart to love him. The lover of God, the one who truly seeks God, is eager that the whole of creation, in accord with the divine will, ascends to him in glory. Through obedience, the monk seeks to be in constant harmony with this movement. Through his prayer services, which Benedict calls the *Opus Dei,* the Work of God, and which modern usage often speaks of as the *Office* or the *Divine Office,* the monk seeks to give voice to this movement, taking care "that our minds are in harmony with our voices." When the monk stands in choir, using the divinely inspired texts and listening to the shared faith of the Fathers, he best expresses and constantly increases his "zeal" for the opus of God, the longing that all that takes place in his life and in the whole of creation be to the glory of the God he loves.

There is no dichotomy or opposition between the liturgical prayer of the monk and nun and their contemplation. "Contemplation" is an interesting word. "Con" means "together with"; "tion" means "being in a state of." "Being in a state of being together with" what? When the priests of pagan Rome wanted to know the will of the gods, they searched the heavens and watched the flight of birds, especially across a particular quadrant they called the *templa.* To know the gods' will one looked to the *templa.* This was projected to the earth; the *templa* became the *templum,* the temple, the place one went to know the gods' will, to be in harmony with the gods. Contemplation then is being in the state of being together with the will of God, with God himself, with the movement of God. The liturgy seeks to bring us into harmony with the movement of God in the creation and the re-creation to bring us into union with God.

The liturgy has its daily and annual cycle. In the daily cycle, the monk completes his day with *Compline,* the completing office or service, and enters into the tomb of sleep. Eager with anticipation—for he is the one who "truly seeks God"—he rises in "the seventh hour of the night," two or three in the morning, or certainly some time before dawn, to await the resurrection of the sun, the daily sacrament of the Incarnation—

Blessed be the Lord, the God of Israel,
for he has visited his people . . .
this by the tender mercy of our God
who from on high will bring the rising Sun to visit us,
to give light to those who live
in darkness and the shadow of death,
and to guide our feet
into the way of peace.

—and of the Resurrection of the Son. The brothers gather in choir and encourage each other with psalmody even as they are encouraged by the Scriptures and the Fathers through their writings. This communal *Vigil* service leads into the silence of solitary watching until the dawn reassembles the monks to sing their *Lauds* in praise of the risen Lord. Today, frequently, the encounter with the risen Lord includes recognizing him in the Breaking of the Bread and entering into Communion with him.

In the third, sixth, and ninth hours—mid-morning, midday, and mid-afternoon—the monk pauses for a moment of reflective psalmody and reading to clarify through these hours of the *Opus Dei—Tierce, Sext,* and *None*—his conscious participation in the opus of God with its ascension to him in glorification.

At the evening "office"—*Vespers*—all gather together to thank the Lord:

My spirit rejoices in God, my Savior
because he has looked upon the lowliness of his servant.
 . . . The Almighty has done great things for me.
Holy is his name.

Then the day and the cycle are ready to enter into completion—*Compline*—once again.

The daily cycle forms the monk and enables him to enter increasingly into a state of harmony with the movement of God in his creation and to participate more fully in contemplation. It also enables him to enter more fully into the *annual cycle* of Salvation History and to draw from those saving mysteries which are the source and object of his contemplation.

Advent is indeed the season for the man who "truly seeks God" as he enters into the longings of the prophets of all the ages. *Christmas* is a birth, even now in his soul, of the fulfillment he seeks. Christ is manifested even more to him in his *Epiphany* and *Baptism*. The purifications of *Lent,* walking with Christ in his journey each day, even down to the hour and minute in *Holy Week,* prepares him for the deeper communion of *Easter* time. When Christ invites him to a higher level of consciousness in the *Ascension,* he opens to receive the Spirit anew at *Pentecost.* He then may enter more fully into the mystery of the "Pilgrim Church" through the long green days of the *Season after Pentecost* till it comes to its consummation in the *Assumption* of Mary and the glorification of *All the Saints* in the *Kingship of Christ,* with *Thanksgiving.* The repeated celebration of these mysteries leads the monk into ever deeper contemplation and out of this contemplation comes a greater celebration of these mysteries. Liturgy and contemplation form an integral whole, each element magnificently nourishing and complementing (in the strictest sense of that word) the other.

This is so provided that these two states are kept in balance. Herein is something of the wisdom of Benedict's *Rule.* In his "school of the Lord's service" he established a harmonious, balanced program of *lectio* and liturgy, with seasonal variations to avoid monotony.

There is really no adequate English word for *lectio;* it has a very special connotation when used in the monastic context. When the monk speaks of *lectio* or *lectio divina,* he is referring to a whole process that the tradition has summed up in the four words *lectio, meditatio, oratio,* and *contemplatio.* Each of these has its special meaning in the tradition:

Lectio, which would be literally translated "reading," certainly does not mean only that. We are speaking of many centuries when most could not read. Saint Basil insisted that his monks learn to read. Saint Benedict did not, but he did insist they memorize a good bit of Scripture and liturgical offices. Reading is the form our *lectio* might most commonly take today, but calling up passages from memory is another form of *lectio*. So is regarding works of art: icons, frescoes, stained-glass windows, as well as the artwork of the greatest of masters—the creation. God reveals himself in and through all of these. If we would, we might best translate *lectio* as "receiving the Revelation of God."

Meditatio traditionally did not mean using the rational mind to penetrate, dissect, and analyze. It meant pondering in its more literal sense of letting the matter weigh quietly within. A word of life drawn from *lectio* would rest in the mind, perhaps more deeply set by repetition, until it sunk into the heart and formed it. "Lord, Lord, Lord," the lips might repeat or just the mind until the heart fell down in adoration.

Oratio is this response of the heart. For the Fathers it usually meant fiery darts of prayer set off by the *meditatio:* "In my meditation fire burst forth."

Abba Paul went to see Abba Basil and said to him, "Abba, as far as I can, I say my little office, I fast a little, I read and meditate, I live in peace and as far as I can, I purify my thoughts. What else can I do?" Then the old man stood up and stretched his hands towards heaven. His fingers became like ten lamps of fire and he said to him, "If you will, you can become all fire. You cannot be a monk unless you become like a consuming fire."

When the darts of fiery prayer become a constant, consuming fire this is *contemplatio*. When under the Holy Spirit the word of *lectio* has so formed the heart that it abides lovingly, wholly in the mystery of the Lord, *oratio* has passed into *contemplatio:* contemplation. This is the goal of all *lectio*. It is a gift. "Prayer should be short and pure," says Saint Benedict, "unless it is prolonged under the inspiration of divine grace."

Saint Benedict's *Rule* allows ample spaces for *lectio*. Depending on where the monk is on his journey and the graces of the particular day, this time will be spent in varying degrees in *lectio, meditatio, oratio,* and *contemplatio*. The aspiration of the heart is always for the *contemplatio.* The Fathers gave counsels and even simple methods to facilitate this. Abba Isaac's method, brought to the West in the fifth century by Saint John Cassian, has enjoyed a new popularity under the name of Centering Prayer. If the monk is attentive to the readings at office (*lectio*) and quietly repeats his prayer word, his word of life (*meditatio*), as he goes about his work, letting aspirations, fiery darts of prayer (*oratio*), ascend to God as they will, then when the time of *lectio* comes he will quickly settle down to enjoy to the full *contemplatio.* Gradually the *contemplatio,* the luminous and captivating presence of God, will become a constant and be the context for all he does. This is the goal of the monastic life, the way to constant prayer.

And it is totally demanding. It means that the self, the false self with which we so readily identify, be wholly consumed as fuel for the fire of the heart. Unfortunately, the monk has repeatedly found ways to escape the demands of true *lectio.* The most obvious has been the classical monastic vice of *acedia,* spiritual sloth. He has not attended to his reading but has given way to what Saint Bernard earmarked as the first degree of pride, *curiositas,* curiosity. He has let his mind and his eyes wander about, looking into everything that is going on, without attending to their deeper meanings—the word of God speaking in and through them. He browses through all the latest books but never ponders their message. This easily leads to other steps of pride: gossip, wit, buffoonery, and meddling, all of which dispose one less and less for *lectio* and leave little time for it.

A more devious because less obvious escape has been an overemphasis on liturgy. Kept in balance liturgy and *lectio,* as we have said, nourish and complement each other. Liturgy not grounded in *lectio* quickly becomes sterile, a boring show even if a very artistic performance. Repeatedly in monastic history this has happened. Benedict pared down the exaggerations of an earlier tradition to a very sober *servitutis pensum*—measure of service. The Cluniac reform which began well enough gradually succumbed until, as Saint Peter Damian remarked, there was hardly a half hour in the day for holy converse. There were extrinsic reasons for this. A Christianized society appreciated the prayer of the monks and nuns and sought to impose upon them through foundations, bequests, and offerings the obligation of even more particular prayers. Office was added to office, and the whole surrounded with countless additional psalms. There was little time left for genuine *lectio* to enkindle *contemplatio*.

The true monastic heart felt this deprivation, and countless monastic reforms of the eleventh and twelfth centuries sought to redress the balance. Most notable were the Cistercians, who strove for an unmitigated return to the simplicity of Benedict's office. Their success, unfortunately, was relatively short-lived. In time they were impelled to add the Office of the Blessed Virgin, the Office of the Dead, the Office of All Saints, penitential processions, and many other prayers.

Today, though, the prevailing escape from the demands of true *lectio* is not in the direction of liturgy. In fact, monks generally have moved towards paring down even Benedict's modest measure. Rather it is the other member of the classical monastic tripartite that has come to dominate and frequently create a harmful imbalance. Both *lectio* and liturgy have been squeezed by labor.

Labora

God planted a garden in Eden and there he put the man he fashioned. God caused to spring up from the soil every kind of tree, enticing to look at and good to eat. . . . God took man and settled him in the garden to look after it and cultivate it. . . . God said to man, "Because you listened to the voice of your wife and ate from the tree of which I had forbidden you to eat, the soil will be cursed. With suffering you will get your food from it all the days of your life. It shall give you brambles and thistles and you shall eat wild plants. With the sweat of your brow you shall earn your bread. . . . God expelled man from the garden of Paradise to till the soil from which he had been taken. He banished the man.

Man and woman were made for Paradise. Their own sin cast them out. As the monk and nun seek the restoration of their lost likeness unto God in his friendship, they seek to return to Paradise. Inspired and empowered by the Lord's prayer: Thy Kingdom come . . . on earth as in heaven, they have sought to make their cloisters a paradise on earth, *paradisus claustralis,* by generously fulfilling man's primary and God-given penance of labor.

60

The site for the abbey of Clairvaux was in the Langres district, not far from the River Aube; the place had for many years been used as a robbers' lair. Of old it was called the Vale of Absinth because wormwood grew there in great abundance. . . .

As I looked about me I thought that I was gazing on a new heaven and a new earth, for it seemed as though there were tracks freshly made by men of our own day in the path that had been first trodden by our fathers, the Egyptian monks of long ago.

This was indeed the golden age of Clairvaux. Virtuous men, who once held honors and riches in the world, lovingly embraced a life of poverty in Christ. And thus they helped plant the Church of God by giving their lives in toil and hardship, in hunger and thirst, in cold and exposure, in insults and persecutions and many difficulties, just like the Apostle Paul. These were the men who made it possible for Clairvaux to enjoy the peace and sufficiency which it has today. . . .

Men who come down from the hills into the valley of Clairvaux for the first time, are struck by the awareness that God dwells there, for the simplicity and unpretentiousness of the buildings in the quiet valley betray the lowly and simple life led by the monks for the sake of Christ. They find that the silence of the deep of nights reigns even in the middle of the day, although in this valley full of men there are no idle souls, and everyone busies himself with the tasks entrusted to him. The only sound that can be heard is the sound of the brethren at work or singing their office in praise of God.

   —Abbot William of Saint Thierry, *Vita primas, Bernardi*

     The early monastic fathers seem to be, as it were, of two minds in regard to work:

Abba Adam and Abba Bitiman visited Abba Achilles. They noticed he had been working the whole night and had woven a great deal. They asked him to say a word to them. He said: "From yesterday evening till now, I have woven twenty mats, although I do not need them; it is for fear God should be angry and accuse me, saying, 'Why did you not work when you could have done so?' This is why I give myself this labor and do as much as I can." They went away greatly edified.

Abba Isaiah said: "Whoever has not worked will not receive a reward from God."

Abba Poemen said: "In Abba Pombo we see three bodily activities: abstinence from food until evening every day, silence, and much manual labor."

A brother said to Abba Pistamon: "If I can get what I need by one means or another, do you still advise me to take the trouble to do manual labor?" The old man replied: "Even if you do have what you need by other means, do not give up your manual labor. Work as much as you can, only do it without getting worried about it."

On the other hand,

Someone questioned Abba Beare in these words: "What shall I do to be saved?" He replied: "Go, reduce your appetite and your manual labor, dwell without care in your cell, and you will be saved."

We find the same ambivalence among the fathers of the golden age. Abbot Guerric of Igny will tell his monks:

In order then, my brethren, that he who loves quiet and bestows it may rest in you, make a point, as the Apostle advises, of being quiet. How will this come about? "I tell you," he says, "to attend to your own business and work with your hands." Work is a load by which our ships are given weight so hearts are given quiet and gravity, and in it the outward man finds a firm foundation and a settled condition.

To achieve the wisdom of continuing in wisdom, it is important, I think, not readily to allow restlessness or any kind of slight provocation to keep you away from any of the exercises of wisdom: the divine office, private prayer, *lectio divina,* the appointed daily labor, or the practice of silence.

Do not then be too sparing of your feet, brothers in the ways of obedience and in the comings and goings which work demands. . . .

William of Saint Thierry writes to the monks of Mont Dieu:

I am at a loss to find a name worthy of them, our Fathers in Egypt and the Thebaid; shall I call them heavenly men or earth bound angels? They lived on earth but their true home was in heaven. They worked with their own hands and fed the poor with the fruits of their toil. While they themselves went hungry, they contributed food from the wastes of the desert to feed the prisons and the hospitals of cities and succored those who were laboring under any form of distress. Yet all this time they lived by the work of their own hands and dwelt in buildings their own hands had erected.

On the other hand, he writes:

Open-air exercises and work not only distract the senses but also often exhaust the spirit, except in the case of heavy field work where great weariness of body leads to contrition and humility of heart. Spiritual exercises should never be laid aside in favor of bodily ones for any length of time nor totally. . . . by bodily exercises in the present context we mean those which involve manual labor.

Maybe I should not say ambivalence but a certain caution and concern for balance and a proper hierarchy of values. "Idleness is the enemy of the soul," wrote Benedict. "Therefore, the brothers should have specified periods for manual labor as well as for *lectio divina.*"

Saint Basil, in his *Long Rules,* offers extensive teaching on work, contained substantially in the responses to six questions. The first, Question 37, lays the solid theological foundations for his teaching on work. Much of it is applicable to all Christians, based as it is on the teaching of the Sacred Scriptures, yet it has specifically monastic dimensions placing the monk's work squarely in the context of his life of prayer. The following chapters display Basil's practicality and wisdom, and address themselves more specifically to the monastic: the sort of work suitable for a monk, as well as how he should act in the business world (Questions 38–40). His final question (42) on the dispositions of the laborer can be readily applied to any Christian life, as can much of the preceding question (41). Both of these, however, underline what is the primary virtue and concern of monastic labor—obedience.

Obedience to the superior and community in the matter of one's work is absolutely fundamental for Saint Basil, yet this is ultimately only a concrete expression of one's obedience to God's will as expressed in the Scriptures. In the course of these six chapters we find forty-four Scripture quotations.

Surprisingly, although Saint Basil does not neglect the important ascetical and penitential aspects of work—for him it involves struggle and great endeavor, fostering the growth of patience and bringing the body into subjection—he does not allude to the primal text of Genesis: "By the sweat of your brow you will earn your bread." The emphasis for this very community-minded Father is on another text altogether: "Be not solicitous for your life, what you shall eat, nor for your body, what you shall put on." Fasting and deprivation are a value to the monk; they open the spaces for greater spiritual hunger. The Christian works that he might have something to give to others, for the other is Christ. Basil does not forbid monks to work to support themselves—he expects them to do it—but in their labors they are to seek to earn, not to make themselves comfortable, but to keep themselves from being a burden to others and to have something with which to help others. All selfishness and self-reliance is set aside. Depending on the Lord, the Christian works for him, in him and in those with whom he identifies himself.

The Apostle's command "to pray without ceasing" and the monk's communal responsibility to gather repeatedly for prayer are not to be used as excuses for holding back from work. The monk, the Christian, is to pray while he works. As he expands on this, Saint Basil gives us some of his most precious teaching on work.

First of all, the Saint is very realistic. Sometimes the monks can pray and recite psalms while they work. Saint Pachomius, with whom Basil was familiar, made elaborate provisions for this. But Basil recognized that sometimes this is not possible, or it is not conducive to edification. It would be forced. In such circumstances, however, the monk could seek to praise God in his heart with psalms, hymns, and spiritual canticles. He could remain conscious of how God is at every moment truly present in his creative love, bringing forth all that is. One could praise God by recognizing that it is he who, at each moment of our labor, is giving our hands the strength to do the task and our minds the knowledge and insight to inspire and direct it. Furthermore, he is present and active in the materials that we are using: both the instruments and the matter. The fully responsive use of these, our own activity, and the ordination of it all to "the good pleasure of God" is the practical way in which we pray constantly.

Saint Basil's attitude toward tools flows from this theological attitude. While we do not find in his *Rule* any statement quite so striking as Saint Benedict's "the tools of the monastery are to be treated as the vessels of the altar"—a statement that invites us to think of our daily labor as the celebration of the Mass of the Universe, a eucharistic transformation of the creation—his teaching is complete and practical. It flows from basic monastic values and principles.

The care of the tools devolves first of all on the worker who uses them. But if he should be negligent, anyone aware of the neglect should remedy it, since the tools are for the good of all. A shovel left out in the path in the rain is everyone's care. Even if it be the tool of another's trade, no one can be indifferent to it. At the same time, the user himself is not to assume a proprietor's attitude toward the tools of his craft. He must allow the superior to use them in any way he wishes. He may not sell or exchange them, or dispose of them in any other way, or acquire others without the superior's blessing. "How could he who has irrevocably chosen not to be master even of his own hands and who has consigned to another the direction of his activity, how could he be consistent in maintaining full authority over the tools of his trade, arrogating to himself the dignity of mastership over them?" This brings to mind Saint Benedict's statement that the monk is no longer master even of his own body.

Saint Basil's lively and insightful faith reconciles the monk's call to constant prayer with responsible labor. He gives a very beautiful and meaningful explanation of the significance of the respective hours of service, and then he approaches the practical question of reconciling this call to prayer with the daily labor.

At the third hour—around 9:00 A.M.—the brethren are to gather together "even if they may have dispersed to the various employments." At this hour they are to recall the gift the Spirit bestowed on the Apostles and so worship that they might be worthy of such sanctity. They are also to implore the guidance and instruction of the Holy Spirit so that all that they do will be good and useful.

Then Saint Basil's moderation and practicality come into play. He realizes that distance or the nature of the work the monks are doing may make it difficult to drop everything and come to the community assembly. In such cases the monks are to consider it a strict obligation to carry out the service where they are and as promptly as they can. The Saint reminds the monks that the Lord is equally present wherever they gather in his name.

Obedience to the Lord—a constant attentiveness to his presence in all—is fundamental in Saint Basil's attitude toward work. In addition, the monk is to attend to his work with enthusiasm, a ready zeal, and careful attention. He is to strive to work blamelessly because he knows that his true, everpresent overseer is none other than the Lord himself.

There is simplicity in Saint Basil. It is an essential quality of monastic life: monk = *monos,* one, simple. The monk is one whose eyes are set blamelessly on the Lord. Saint Basil's simplicity is reflected here in another way. He counsels the laborer to set himself with constancy to one task and not move about, now busy at one kind of task, now at another. "We are incapable by nature of following successfully a number of pursuits at the same time; to finish one task with diligent care is more beneficial than to undertake many. . . ." But as always, Saint Basil's moderation prevails. If necessity requires it, and one has the ability, he can lend his brother a hand, ". . . . just as, in the case of our bodily members, we support ourselves with the hand when the foot is limping."

In the course of three chapters Saint Basil lays down many practical provisions in regard to the monk's work. In Question 38 he asks: What sort of trades are suitable to the monastic profession? His principles here are excellent and equally valid for our times.

A monk wants to live a life that is in constant attendance on the Lord. Therefore, in choosing his work he should seek that which allows him a tranquil and undisturbed life, a livelihood marked with simplicity and frugality. It should be an employment for which he will be able to get the necessary materials and tools without great difficulty, be able to sell the products readily, and will not have to get involved in unsuitable or harmful relations. His product should not pamper the foolish and harmful desires of men. Basil suggests such crafts as weaving, shoemaking, carpentry, and metal work. He illustrates his last point from these trades. The weaver should make things that will serve daily life and not fancy things to trap and ensnare the young. The shoemaker should seek to satisfy real needs.

For Saint Basil farming is the most desirable type of employment. It produces immediate necessities and is in accordance with the other conditions he has laid down. Farmers do not have to go about much, and it is good for monks to stay in one place. Such stability is seemly and beneficial; it is productive of mutual edification; and it fosters faithful observance.

Saint Basil was as concerned about the monks' travel as Saint Benedict, who wanted all necessities to be as much as possible within the enclosure of the monastery. But here again Basil shows his moderation and wisdom. It would be better to stay home and lower prices to attract customers to the monastery, but he realizes this cannot always be done. He recognizes that monks will have to go out to the market, but they are not to go about as peddlers. When they go out he urges them to travel in groups, to go to places that are not far distant where they can stay with devout people, and to stay together. These guidelines not only provide support for their spiritual life; they also provide mutual protection: difficult and avaricious men will be slow to take advantage of one in the presence of others. Saint Basil also notes that the monks should not try to sell their wares at shrines, capitalizing on the piety of the pilgrim. Shrines are for pilgrimage and prayer only, not for trafficking. Christ's action in the Temple is proof enough for this.

Basically, Basil opposes traveling, or anything else that can weaken or rupture the unity among the brethren. He does want men to use their talents, but only with the blessing of the community. Saint Benedict also agreed. One should not exercise a craft or learn a new one without a blessing, nor should he refuse to learn one when asked. For Saint Basil, community, unity in fraternity, is of major importance. Christian community can only be founded on obedience, obedience to the Gospels, to God, and to the legitimate authority, the expression of God's direction, at the center of the community.

Saint Basil does not say anything about intellectual labors or apostolic ministry outside the monastery, nor does Benedict or early monastic Fathers in general. Yet men like Evagrius Ponticus produced their *Chapters on Prayer,* and soon enough monks like Saint Bede the Venerable were devoting most if not all their work time to study and writing. Even among the early Cistercians who placed such emphasis on manual labor, we find Saint Stephen Harding studying Hebrew with a Rabbi and translating the Bible and other Fathers engaged in extensive writing, even of a secular nature.

In Ireland from the earliest times there was a close bond between sacerdotal ministry and monastery. The dioceses were centered in the abbeys. Soon missionary monks set forth on the work of evangelization. There were precedents for this, in Saint Anselm's mission to Britain and earlier in Anthony the Great's journeys to Alexandria to minister to the Christians there. What was distinctive, though, was that monastic missionaries usually quickly established monasteries to serve as centers for their work, support the missionaries in their labors, and be models of Christian community and prayer.

Today monks continue in all these forms of work. In some orders and monasteries manual labor is held in high esteem; and apostolic work, especially outside the monastery, is shunned. This is almost universally true of nuns and true of those monks who seek the greatest freedom for the flowering of the contemplative dimension of life. Many monasteries, though, engage in parochial and missionary work; not a few conduct schools at the monastery itself. The compatibility of some of these endeavors is debated. The Second Vatican Council recognizes the legitimacy of some such occupations. In its decree *On the Adaptation and Renewal of Religious Life* it first spoke of "communities which are totally dedicated to contemplation," and then went on to speak of monastic life, indicating that monks could be committed entirely to a life of worship or could take up some apostolate:

In the East and in the West, the venerable institution of monastic life should be faithfully preserved and should grow ever-increasingly radiant with its own authentic spirit. Through the long course of centuries, this institution has proved its merits splendidly to the Church and to human society. The main task of monks is to render to the Divine Majesty a service at once simple and noble, within the monastic confines. This they do either by devoting themselves entirely to divine worship in a life that is hidden or by lawfully taking up some apostolate or works of Christian charity. While safeguarding the proper identity of each institution, let monasteries be renewed in their ancient and beneficial traditions and so adapt them to modern needs of souls that monasteries will be seedbeds of growth of the Christian people.

Certainly the cautions of the fathers with regard to the danger of overdoing manual labor, are even more applicable to these apostolic works, which tend to be even more engrossing. The primacy of prayer, the space for true *lectio,* must always be maintained, and so must the common life of the monks, to which we now turn our attention.

Vita Communis

Saint Bernard of Clairvaux is notorious for the statement *Vita communis poenitentia maxima,* "Community, my greatest penance." Certainly one does not need to read very extensively to discover that the "angelic life," as monastic life has sometimes been called, includes some fallen—or at least very human—angels. Fathers could rhapsodize about the life. Saint Aelred (abbot from 1142–1167) becomes quite poetical as he describes it:

The day before yesterday, when I was going round the cloister of the monastery, then sitting with the brethren in a loving circle, as though amid the delights of paradise, I admired the leaves, the flowers, and the fruit of every tree. I found no one in that great number whom I did not love, and whom I did not believe loved me. I was filled with such a joy as passes all the delights of this world. For I felt as though my spirit was transfused into them all, and their affection into me, so that I could say with the prophet: "Behold how good and how pleasant it is for brethren to dwell together in unity."

However Aelred's biographer recounts another scene, one that finds Aelred weak and infirm:

And, as we two sat alone in the room, a monk entered, mad with rage, a real wild bull in full charge. He came upon Aelred, bellowing and grimacing, seized his mat and jerked it up with the father on it and hurled this father of a hundred monks and five hundred lay brothers into the fire among the coals, shouting: "You wretch, now I am going to kill you. . . ."

That sounds more like purgatory than paradise. As we read Saint Bendict's *Rule for Monasteries* with its many penal prescriptions, even beatings, for those "who are evil or stubborn, arrogant or disobedient" and its chapter forbidding the brethren from hitting each other, we begin to sense that even in monasteries where men are not allowed easy entrance, the monks are in the process of conversion. Monks have their weaknesses, even their lapses into malice; and they certainly have their idiosyncrasies. Forgiveness is a very integral part of every Christian life: Forgive us as we forgive. Living side by side, in relatively close quarters day in and day out, year after year, can be *poenitentia maxima*. But monks strive for the better and often enough attain it.

The holy monks of whom we speak, if made superiors, acquit themselves of their office with all solicitude, and are like fathers to their sons. But if they are made subject to others, then they obey with humility and are like sons to their fathers. If they are obliged to live with others, they do so with charity. If they live in community, they make themselves the servants of all. They are lovingly inclined towards everyone, and live in peaceful agreement about all that is good. They come together with joy, and go out of their way to show charity towards one another. To those who are below them in any way, they show a tender affection in their deeds. On their elders they bestow love to the point of subjection. To those above them their obedience goes as far as complete service. They do not seek their own interests, but those of the brethren. Whenever possible they make the common good their own, in spite of detriment to themselves. For they have received that pledge which is the Holy Spirit's gift, and they know that bodily service will soon pass into the adoption of those who will be revealed as the sons of God. Therefore they find it easy to bend both body and will to whatsoever thing the greatest of commandments orders.

—Abbot William of St. Thierry

Aelred tells a novice: If out in the world you did what you do here, men would hold you a saint. But here you are lost in the crowd. Indeed, it would be heroic, outside, on one's own, to rise each day in the early hours to spend those hours in prayer. But in the monastery, where no television or gab session keeps one up late, where everyone else rises early and supports each other in prayer and watching, it is easy enough. It is not easy to rise at three A.M.—nature herself is in deepest rest—but because of the way the profound quietness of those hours supports deep prayer, experience begins to make it more attractive, and the development of good habit can further support it. To live in a community of like-minded brothers, sharing a common goal, and using common means together is immensely supportive.

When a man is first drawn to the monastic life, he usually has very high ideals, and he is very apt to idolize the monks. When he enters the monastery, or very soon thereafter, he comes into contact with the way things really are in the monastery: flesh-and-blood, sinful men struggling with everyday life. What he sees may be very distant from the ideal. He is now confronted with a choice. He can cling to his ideal, reject the real, and go off in an endless search for the ideal monastery, the ideal community, the ideal monks. Or he may decide to be "realistic," give up his ideals, and settle for what is real. At first this way may seem easy, but in the end it is very frustrating; life goes nowhere, so why stay? Or he may decide to keep his ideals and lovingly embrace the real in himself and others and move gently but persistently toward the ideal. His life is invigorated by a dynamic tension. He is going somewhere. And he is not going alone. He is helping others and being helped by them. His vision is being confirmed and supported.

Some monks prefer smaller communities. They find large ones too impersonal. How can you know forty or fifty, not to mention a hundred or more brothers intimately and really share with them? Large communities tend to be more formal and structured. They tend to possess more and have more to care for, for they must support more people. In a smaller community, life can be more immediate, simple, and poor.

On the other hand, some monks prefer large communities. Thomas Merton was such a monk. A large community offers greater freedom than a small community where everyone must be present almost all the time to keep things going. In a large community monks can take turns, dividing up chores and providing back-up service for each other. If some, or even many, are absent life goes on.

Considering the vow of stability in community of the Benedictine tradition, a novice must discern in which monastic community he can best grow as a lover. Community size with its relative freedom or intimacy is an important factor, as well as the style of the spiritual father(s) and the observance, the degree of uniformity or pluralism, and the climate, both literal and metaphorical.

The strictly eremitical life remains an exceptional vocation. It is provided.for in the new Code of Canon Law. It is lived in dependence upon a bishop or a religious superior;

the hermit remains a part of the Church. It is probably most easily lived within a monastic domain in dependence on a monastic father or mother. But where the Spirit is, there is freedom. There are hermits, men and women, in the deserts of our cities.

Most who are drawn to an eremitical style of life find the support of others in a laura (there are a few in existence now) or an eremitical order such as the Carthusians or Camaldolese provides the best context for them. The common life is greatly reduced in these groups, but it is present in a common domain, a common basic rule, some common exercises together, some common services, and a common purse. Most important there is the regular, if limited, contact and committed communion with brothers or sisters.

This is what is at the heart of all common life: community, communion, a bonding in unity, union, love. A common life without it is hell—quite literally! Common life can be very demanding, a *poenitentia maxima* calling for the constant availability of not only all that one has—material and spiritual resources—but all that one is. It is a school of love, a school of compassion. It is to be taken seriously, but not too seriously. There needs to be time for play, time to enjoy one's friends and brothers, and time to waste on each other. And one hopes to find among those brothers, whether they be few or many, that special friend:

It is such a joy to have the consolation of someone's affection—someone to whom we are deeply united by the bonds of love, someone in whom our weary spirit may find rest, and to whom we may pour out our souls . . . someone whose conversation is as sweet as a song in the tedium of our daily life. He is one whose soul will be to us a refuge to creep into when the world is altogether too much for us, someone to whom we can confide all our thoughts. His spirit will give us the comforting kiss that heals all the sickness of our preoccupied hearts. He will weep with us when we are troubled, and rejoice with us when we are happy; he will always be there to consult when we are in doubt. We will be so deeply bound to him in our hearts that even when he is far away, we will find him together with us in the spirit, together and alone. The world will fall asleep around us, we will find, and our souls will be at rest, embraced in absolute peace. Our two hearts will be quiet together, united as if they were one, as the grace of the Holy Spirit flows over us both.   —Abbot Aelred of Rievaulx

The common life does not rule out particular friendships. In fact, it cultivates and fosters the growth of those dispositions and virtues necessary for true friendship. The history of monasticism is marked by the stories of true friends.

Thus far my discussion has drawn largely from only one particular tradition, that of Western Christian monasticism, with contributions from its sources in Eastern Christianity. That tradition is an expression of a much broader and more ancient stream; in fact, monasticism is found in almost all the great religions of the world. But monastic life also expresses a dimension that should be present in every fully developed human life.

In 1977 I convened a meeting of monastics to form a World Monastic Council to initiate and support dialogue among monks and nuns of different religious traditions, East and West. As preparations progressed and news of the planned meeting became more widely disseminated, two surprises emerged.

The first was a request from the United Nations to send a representative to our meeting. Dr. Robert Muller, special assistant to the UN Secretary General, who had been with the United Nations since its inception, proved to be one of the meeting's most enthusiastic participants. He suggested that the World Monastic Council be established as a nongovernmental organization (NGO) within the United Nations, an organization that, having initially devoted its energy almost exclusively to political and economic issues—one must live and eat before one can do anything else—had begun to concern itself with the ethics that undergird human collaboration. Some fourteen ethical codes have been established and elaborated by the United Nations in the course of the last decade, and the last few years have witnessed a growing awareness among that world assembly that the ethical foundations of human solidarity must be grounded in and enlivened by a recognition of the spiritual unity of human kind—a recognition that flows from some kind of inner personal experience. That it be monks and nuns of the world who reach out to each other and begin to express in some concrete way this spiritual basis for global solidarity is logical, to say the least. Indeed, it is but an expression of their inner experience of the essential oneness of all creation. When the Disarmament Conference of the United Nations convened in June of 1982, it was estimated that there were over one thousand monks and nuns present, supporting the assembly by their silent but powerful meditation. Today, more urgently than ever before, monastic pray-ers are called forth to work for true peace by seeking to create among themselves and those around them a strong awareness that we are in fact one global *community*.

The second surprise that emerged as we prepared for our 1977 meeting was the desire of a large number of lay persons to be present. We were inclined at first to call them nonmonastic participants but, as one of their number boldly affirmed to Thomas Merton at Santa Barbara on the eve of Merton's fatal journey East, they are monks too. We had to recognize what they strongly affirmed in regard to the monasticism of the laity. The basic elements of monastic life that I have spoken of in this chapter quite definitely have their place in the life of the laity. Today there is not only a growing recognition of that fact but a widely expressed desire—and actual movement—toward lessening the gap between monks and nuns and those faithful who have not gone apart.

Many of the faithful have turned toward monasteries for help in re-establishing that contemplative dimension, which has largely fallen out of the lived experience of an active Christian church. Today monks and nuns, to the degree that they have been faithful to the tradition that has handed down this practice from generation to generation, are able once again to teach Centering Prayer, the Prayer of the Heart, as their spiritual fathers and mothers of old did right up to the time of the Reformation. In an increasingly frentic secular environment, the need to be able to enter into contemplative prayer and find one's own center in the ground of being who is our God has become more and more urgent; in the experience of many, it is essential to preserving one's true humanity. In a materialistic world where the current flows so strongly in so many dehumanizing directions, families have sought to establish supportive bonds with other, like-minded families. In some cases this has led to the formation of such groups as the Families of Saint Benedict, family groups that draw their inspiration and guidance from the ancient monastic rules and that usually seek affiliation with and spiritual support from an established monastic community.

Another response to this need for centering in God has been the development of an expanded concept of monastic community. This emerging ideas is not wholly new; it would find strongly evocative precedent in the medieval towns that grew up around such monasteries as Cluny. While many of the church renewal movements of the twelfth century sought to discourage this close relationship, it was common in the immediately preceding centuries and continued to a lesser degree through the succeeding centuries. Families settled in the shadows of the abbey walls so that the men could find work in the monks' fields and shops and the women, occasionally, in their poultry yards and laundries. There was medical care to be had in the monastery, and sustenance in times of need. Monastic shops produced candles, clothes, shoes; the bakeries, bread; and the cellars, wine and cheese—all of which the monks shared with the people. Most important, the constant prayers of the monks poured out over the people and at due times and seasons the faithful could join the monks at their prayers, masses, and religious festivals. Finally, each person could hope to rest near the holy monks and the relics they venerated as they awaited the resurrection.

The totality of this configuration is not likely to be reproduced in modern times, although in some cases—such as Our Lady of Guadalupe Abbey, Pecos, New Mexico—it is to a surprising degree. More typical of today is the monastic community of concentric circles, usually located in or near a city. At the core of such a community is a fully commited monastic group, but living with those monks or nuns are lay persons, often of both sexes, sharing fully in their community life. Sometimes such lay members continue to work outside the monastery to help support the monastic family, but in other instances their work lies within the community. Additional lay people live outside the monastery, singly or in small groups; they commit themselves to help support the monastic community and, more important, to join the rest of the community at the regular prayer services and other community functions. Finally, there are those whose bond is more peripheral, not unlike that of the oblates of more traditional monasteries—a bond of prayer, occasional visits that afford time and space for solitude, and voluntary support.

These monastic communities of concentric circles are becoming powerful focal points of prayer and, through their deep insertion into the local Christian community, express well the monastic core that should be at the heart of every vital Christian life. Whether such communities will prove to be a passing phenomenon of our times or come to be a common enlivening feature within the emerging renewed Church remains to be seen. They do make new demands on and bring extensive enriching possibilities into the monastic community. How the monks and nuns in the core community are to express and experience the essential monastic apartness is a provoking challenge. Whether in the end these communities are able to remain monastic in any truly identifiable sense is questionable, but as I noted, there is the historical precedent of medieval monasticism. For some monasteries such change may become necessity—the only adequate solution to an evolving social situation that on the one hand locates them beside a busy road that brings multitudes to their former solitude and on the other hand forces them into increasing dependence on public services (electricity, water, fire and police protection, and so on) and financial support. To allow the physical and material bonding to be more significant than the spiritual would do violence to monastic values and witness. Undoubtedly these new expressions of monastic community will undergo further evolution as they enliven the monastic dimension in the lives of more and more of the faithful, sharing with them their life of prayer and their attitudes toward work.

Christianity is at root a community life. So it is described in the Acts of the Apostles:

The faithful all lived together and owned everything in common; they sold their goods and possessions (remember the Great Anthony) and shared out the proceeds among themselves according to what each one needed. They went as a body to the Temple every day . . . , they shared their food gladly and generously. . . . The whole group of believers was united, heart and soul. . . . None of their members was ever in want. . . .

Christian monasticism has sought to live this ideal as literally as possible.

Let us look now at the more recent stages of monasticism's pilgrim journey.

COMMUNITY

"Community is always poised between two poles: solitude and togetherness. Without togetherness community disperses; without solitude community collapses into a mass, a crowd."—Brother David Steindl-Rast, O.S.B.

84

3.

In Our Time

It would be difficult to say when the medieval golden age of monasticism turned silver. Nor could one easily catalogue all the causes. Diminution of numbers had something to do with it, although the Carthusians, who were never numerous, remained steadfast in their adhesion to their ideals. All their monasteries have never housed more than a total of five hundred monks in post-Reformation times, yet they have been faithful. The loss of numbers among the Cistercians and other congregations coming out of the Gregorian Reform had a more serious effect. First, with the vitality of their reform and later, their power, these monasteries acquired vast land holdings. The care of these was entrusted to capable and devoted lay brothers.

The lay brotherhood opened a place for the common man in what had become a clericalized monastic world. It was definitely a second class place (the Second Vatican Council had the courage in 1965 to order an end of this class system in monasteries), but one that in the twelfth century met the needs and aspirations of a great number of men. In the following century it would be the new, fervent mendicant orders of friars—the Franciscans and Dominicans—who would attract great numbers from among the common folk, while the monks in the traditional monasteries increasingly had to manage their own temporal affairs.

In addition, the Church did not hesitate to mine the monasteries to find capable and holy men to serve its more active needs. Many monastic leaders were called forth to serve as bishops and legates, cardinals and even popes. The monks for their part were responsive and even became ambitious. Monastic houses of study or colleges were established at the great universities in Paris and Oxford, and men were sent there for years of study after only a minimal monastic formation and experience. The result was scholarly clerics in monastic habits. While the grace of conversion may come to a man rather suddenly and create in him almost instantaneously a deep and profound change, it takes time to absorb the wisdom of a monastic heritage and to experience its deeper meaning in a loving union with God and his people. In all likelihood many of those entering the monasteries in this period of decline had not undergone an intitial conversion and entered for less than ideal reasons. The wealth of the monasteries did offer security, at least until it was depleted or despoiled by absent abbots or rapacious rulers, ecclesiastical and secular.

The Black Death took its toll, too, within the cloisters as well as among the communities from which new recruits would have come. If the nuns were not as affected by the call to more active involvement in the Church and the world, they were greatly affected by this plague as well as by the rapacity of the powers around them. Regarding women, there is less data, but the new medicant orders of friars did establish what have been called "second orders" for women. These drew candidates who might have joined the established monastic orders, but in fact women in these orders lived a fully monastic life. As far as the women were concerned, the Church lost nothing in regard to its monastic dimension. The popularity and omnipresence of the friars probably encouraged an increase in vocation to the cloister on the part of women. Only in the eighteenth and nineteenth centuries did the possibility of an active religious life for women emerge in the Church. Till then the nun who had an active influence outside of her cloister was exceptional, although there were significant exceptions.

At the heart of the Church there is an ever renewing source, the Holy Spirit, the source of all life and love. Through him the Church is continually renewed, as is monasticism, which is close to the heart of the Church. The fifteenth century saw the beginning of monastic congregations that sought to do what the great monastic reforms of the tenth, eleventh, and twelfth centuries had done. In these associations of monasteries, where abbots met regularly in supportive, fraternal chapters, and visiting abbots or teams challenged communities to examine periodically their fidelity, the monk and the autonomous monastery were offered a compatible support system. Exaggerated emphasis on enclosure as well as male domination basically withheld this support system from nuns until recent decades.

In the first days of the fifteenth and seventeenth centuries this structural renewal was a seed sown for the future. Destructive events such as the Protestant Reformation wiped out most of the monasteries in northern Europe and the British Isles. The French revolutionary forces and secularization in Spain and Portugal continued the devastation. The flowering of new Christian peoples in Latin America did give rise to some new monasteries, but they were very few compared to the great number lost in Europe. In addition, forces like Josephism in Austria—which compelled monks to replace members of the suppressed religious orders in the active mission of the Church—as well as general worldliness and destitution, undermined the possibility of living a vital, communal monastic life.

The congregational seed sown earlier, however, sprang up in the nineteenth century. The labors of extraordinary founders like Dom Proper Guéranger at Solesmes, Pietro Casaretto at Subiaco, and the Wolter brothers at Beuron, as well as other courageous pioneers and exiles, led to the birth of numerous monastic congregations on both sides of the Atlantic. The emphases of these new and renewed congregations varied. In the "new world" they often took an active bent; there was much to do in a pioneer Church made up largely of immigrants. The strength of the monastic dimension among these monks and nuns seems to have depended on the depth of the monastic experience of the founders. In England the monks were fully part of the struggle of an excised Church to replant itself. On the continent the new congregations were strong in their emphasis on the basic monastic values. The role of liturgical celebration in the life of prayer received greatest emphasis in the Solesmes Congregation; the Trappists emphasized asceticism and contemplation. Some of these congregations have remained primarily national while others embraced monasteries in many nations.

The phenomenon of the most recent decades has been the outreach to all nations. Many new monasteries have been started in the United States and Latin America. Christian monastic communities have sprung up in all parts of Africa, dot southern and eastern Asia, and reach down through the Pacific islands to Australia and New Zealand. Everywhere the ancient monastic heritage seeks to adapt itself and incorporate, insofar as it can, something of the richness of the local culture: its language, symbols, music, and rituals, as many threads as possible from its fabric of life.

Perhaps the best known of all these new ventures are two Catholic ashrams in southern India. In 1939 Father Jules Monchanin, a priest of Lyons, set out for the subcontinent to labor in the diocese of Tiruchirapalli. About ten years later he was joined by a Benedictine, Father Henri Le Saux, a monk from the Abbey of Saint Anne de Kergonan in Brittany, and on the feast of Saint Benedict, March 21, 1950, they inaugurated an ashram on the banks of the Kavery, the sacred river of South India, just outside of Kulitalai. Their aim was

to form the first nucleus of a monastery (or rather a *laura,* a gouping of neighboring anchorites like the ancient laura of Saint Sabas in Palestine) which is founded on the *Rule of Saint Benedict. . . .* And the monastery will be Indian style. We would like to crystalize and transubstantiate the search of the Hindu *sannyasi* [renunciate]. This means that we must grasp the authentic Hindu search for God in order to Christianize it. . . .

In 1957 Monchanin died, and Le Saux, who had adopted the Indian name of Abishiktananda, retired to a more solitary life in the Himalayas. In the meantime a Belgian Trappist and an English Benedictine, inspired with the same vision, had begun another ashram. Father Bede Griffiths, the Benedictine, then left Father Francis Archarya to care for their ashram at Kurisumala in the mountains of Kerala while he descended to the banks of the Kavery to continue the work of Monchanin and Le Saux at Shantivanam.

These two ashrams, which have attracted a steadily increasing flow of visitors from all parts of the Christian world as well as from India, have inspired many similar attempts, not only in India but elsewhere. An ashram in Kansas, for example, has taken over the name Shantivanam. Another founded in Oklahoma by a nun who lived at the Kulitalai ashram for some time is called Forest of Peace, which is the English translation for Shantivanam. A Japanese Dominican, Father Shigeto Oshida, made a similar attempt to "transubstantiate" (to use Monchanin's term) Zen Buddhist tradition and practice in a Christian monastic community at Takamori.

These transcultural outreaches—and there are others, such as Larva Netofa in Galilee, which integrates the surrounding Jewish and Aramaic traditions—inaugurate one of the courses monastic evolution will take as we advance in global solidarity and Catholicism becomes more catholic.

Most new monasteries are foundations of the great orders: the Benedictines and Cistercians, the Camaldolese and the Carthusians. A recent phenomenon, however, is the number of monasteries that draw from the common monastic heritage but seek a new and independent expression. A parallel to this is found in the eleventh- and twelfth-century monastic revival. It is not a vain hope that some of these new monastic experiments will flourish and have a progeny comparable to Cîteaux and La Grande Chartreuse.

Besides these small, simplified communities and the eremitical ventures which are easily identifiable as traditionally monastic, there are new congregations such as the Little Brothers and the Little Sisters founded in the spirit of Charles de Foucauld. These communities maintain traditional roots and practices, but establish their houses in the new deserts within the cities. Prayer and hospitality are the marks of their lives; they earn their living working among and with the poorest. Whether such urban monasticism is validly called *monastic* is still disputed. Convents have long found their place within cities, but nuns have usually been cut off from their surroundings by high walls, grills, and other artificial means. These new groups, who are having their influence on the older ones, depend on the simplicity and poverty of prayer-filled lives to set them apart from the pressing world around them. The small numbers in their local communities—usually two or three—and the centralization of their congregations (which allows for the members to be moved freely from one community to another) also differentiates them from the more common monastic tradition.

The existence of these new movements, along with the increase of traditional monasteries of all sizes, varying emphases, and degrees of austerity, offers the Catholic man or woman attracted to the monastic life today challenging decisions. Vocations to the monastic life are certainly on the increase. The popular writings of the Cistercian monk, Thomas Merton (Father M. Louis of Gethsemani Abbey, Kentucky), translated into many languages, continue to be widely read. Many other monks and nuns have published also, including Father Raymond of Gethsemani, Dom Bede Griffiths, Sister Mary Francis of Roswell, Dom Jean Leclercq, Father Thomas Keating, and many others. Innumerable television shows and magazine and newspaper articles have featured monks and nuns and their way of life. The widespread immigration of Hindu and Buddhist monks to Western Europe and the United States have not only attracted Christians to their ashrams and meditation centers, but have sent them searching into their own monastic heritage. Almost every Catholic monastery has some novice or young religious who first met the monastic life in an Eastern form.

These same influences have touched the other Christian churches in varying degrees. Within the Anglican Church the restoration of monastic life began earlier, in nineteenth-century England, with such groups as the Society of Saint John the Evangelist (the Cawley Fathers) and the Sisters of the Love of God, both at Oxford. A Benedictine monastery for men flourishes at Nashdom and now has a daughterhouse in the United States at Three Rivers, Michigan, and another beginning in Australia. At West Malling, Kent, there is a large abbey of Benedictine nuns.

The struggle to re-establish monastic life has not been as difficult in this Church, which kept much of its Catholic heritage, as it has been in the Reformed Churches. The Monastery at Taizé in France stands out, but there are other monastic endeavors in the Reformed tradition: Grandchamp, Pomeyral, and the Marienschwestern of Darmstadt. These have had to confront the positions taken by the sixteenth-century Reformers in regard to monasticism, vows, and celibacy. Taizé has not only sent out small fraternities to all parts of the world and called forth a powerful response from young people, but has become a truly ecumenical brotherhood. Today more than twenty-five percent of the brothers are Roman Catholic. They live a full communal life with Protestants from many churches.

Among Orthodox Christians monasticism has remained very much at the heart of the Churches. Seventeenth-century Russia experienced a tension very similar to that in Catholic Europe in the twelfth century between a monasticism centered very much on ritual and liturgy and a more simple monastic life geared towards hysechasm or contemplative prayer. Saint Joseph of Volotsky, with the backing of the imperial Court, wrote the last great Russian rule, drawing, like Saint Athanasius of the Great Laura, in some small measure on *The Rule of Saint Benedict*. Saint Nil, who did not enjoy such court favor, drew his teaching from the richness of the Desert Fathers. (The writings of Evagrius Ponticus found favor among the Orthodox under the name of Saint Nil.) Secular authority, especially in the Byzantine states where Church and state were so closely intertwined, always preferred a more regulated and less mystical monasticism, which is easier to control. At different periods, especially during the counter-Reformation, the authority of the Roman Catholic Church has displayed the same tendency.

Orthodox monasticism—which managed not only to survive but remain vital under centuries of Moslem domination—has not faltered under atheistic Communist regimes. While these governments have closed many monasteries and restricted recruitment in most of the others, spiritual fathers have continued to tonsure (the term used for the rite consecrating a monastic) thousands of monks and nuns who live a monastic life as best they can in the midst of a secular society. Spiritual fathers and mothers have emigrated and established new monasteries in Western Europe and America, bringing with them the art of the Jesus Prayer and other hesychast practices. In the last decades, life in the monastic republic of Mount Athos has experienced a new flowering under the paternal guidance of a number of relatively young spiritual fathers: Father Paiseos, Archimandrite Vasileios, Archimandrite Aimilianos, and others. The same men have also fathered flourishing convents of nuns in other parts of Greece.

There was in one of the American monasteries an old lay brother by the name of Patrick. He was the last of the Irish immigrants. As the years went by, his eyesight began to fail. But each day old Patrick would seek out the daily newspaper and read the headlines that stood out in bold black print. These were the concerns of his prayers for the next twenty-four hours. In the course of history individual monks and nuns have played dramatic roles as peacemakers. Since the days the Desert Fathers sent boat loads of grain down the Nile to Alexandria's starving poor, they have dramatically or quietly responded to the social needs around them. But always they have prayed, in the day and in the night. The power and significance of that intercession some have denied or questioned; but the Church has always affirmed it, inspired by the example and word of its Founder, who spent his nights in prayer and said: "Ask and you shall receive."

Today there is a renewed awareness of the importance and power of intercessory prayer, as well as of another dimension of contemplation: the leaven in the dough which leavens the whole. The solidarity of the human family, of the one Christ, is such that whenever one member rises to a new level of consciousness he or she lifts up all others. Never has there been such need and urgency for transformation of consciousness. It is unknown in the history of peoples and nations for weapons to have been stockpiled and not used. But if we use the weapons we now have stockpiled, there will probably be no one left to record the consistency. There must be a change of pattern, a transformation of consciousness so grounded in an awareness of human solidarity that the use of destructive weapons becomes unthinkable. Monks and nuns of all the great religions, all around the globe, in their cells at night, in their chanting by day, seek higher levels of consciousness, "truly seek God," as the Father of Western monasticism phrased it. In this they find themselves creating an ever greater solidarity with all their brothers and sisters everywhere, thus becoming a powerful force for the peace and well-being of the human family in our time.

Chronology

285

Saint Anthony the Great, sixteen years after hearing the call to the ascetic life, withdraws into the desert and lives on as the "Father of Monks" until his death in 356.

323

Saint Pachomius (ca.292–346), settling in Tabennesi, establishes a monastic community that was to grow until at the time of his death there were some 5,000 monks divided among several monasteries.

ca. 330

Monasteries begin to develop in Palestine.

341

Saint Anthony finds Saint Paul of Thebes, who had retired into the desert ninety years earlier, probably the same year Anthony was born. Paul dies and is buried in a secret place by Anthony.

357

Saint Athanasius, Archibishop of Alexandria (†373), writes the *Life of Anthony,* which, especially in Evagrius' translation, had a great impact on future monastic development. Athanasius' periods of exile in the West led to the establishment of the first monastic centers in Rome, Treves, north Italy, and Aquileia.

Saint Basil, later called the Great (†379), is baptized and sets off to visit monks in Syria and Egypt. On his return he established cenobitic life in Cappodocia and wrote the *Long* and *Short Rules* (370), which were to inspire much of Byzantine monasticism and that of the West, through Saint Benedict of Nursia.

372

Saint Martin of Tours, leaving his hermitage at Ligugé, founds Marmoutier and becomes the model monk-bishop of Gaul.

378

The widow Saint Melania, called the Elder (342−ca.409), after disposing of her wealth, establishes a double monastery (for monks and nuns), in Jerusalem. She later attends to the upbringing of her granddaughter of the same name, Melania the Younger (383−439), who in her turn founds a convent for nuns on the Mount of Olives (432) and a monastery for monks nearby (436). Both Melanias are influenced by Saint Paulinus of Nola, Rufinus, and Saint Augustine of Hippo.

ca. 383

Evagrius Ponticus (345−399) arrives in Nitria and the Cells in the Egyptian desert. Through this gifted writer, ancient monastic wisdom, both theoretical and practical, has been transmitted to all succeeding generations.

ca. 390

The death of Saint Macarius the Egyptian, who first gathered disciples in the great desert of Scete, south of Nitria.

396

Meropius Paulinus (ca.353−431), after distributing his immense wealth, together with his wife Therasia, with whom he had embraced sexual abstinence, arrives at Nola, where they establish a house-monastery. Saint Paulinus was related to or in touch with almost every significant monastic figure of the time and had a great influence. His many *carmina* and letters give us a candid view of an emerging Western monasticism.

404

Saint Jerome (345−420), who spent most of his monastic life in Bethlehem translating and commenting on sacred Scripture, translates the *Pachomian Rule* into Latin. Earlier, he wrote *The Life of Paul of Thebes* (ca. 379) and *The Life of Saint Hilarion* (390).

ca. 410

Saint Honoratus (†430) and his kinsman, Hilary, settle on the island of Lérins off the coast of Cannes to inaugurate a monastic community whose importance in transmitting the monastic heritage of the East to Europe cannot be exaggerated. Among its members and visitors were innumerable important and saintly monastic figures such as Caesarius of Arles, the monastic lawgiver; Vincent of Lérins, the early theologian; Patrick, the apostle of Ireland; and Augustine, the first archbishop of Canterbury. Lérins went through periods of suppression under the Saracens (732−975) and hostile governments, but flourishes today. It was affiliated to the Cistercian order in 1515 and is today the center of the Congregation of Senanque.

ca. 424–435

Saint John Cassian—a Dalmatian (†435) who studied at Rome, traveled widely in the East, and then founded two monasteries near Marseilles—writes twelve books of customs, *Institutiones,* which detail and adapt the cenobitic life of Egypt, and twenty-four conferences, *Collationes,* which impart its inner spirit. His writings have had extensive influence on Western monasticism both directly and through Benedict of Nursia.

ca. 480

The birth of Saint Benedict of Nursia. As a young man he fled from the allure of Rome and lived in a hidden cave for three years. After an unsuccessful attempt to establish a peaceful monastic life at Subiaco, he moved his community to Monte Cassino (529) where he died around 547. His *Rule for Monasteries* has become normative for most of Western monasticism.

483

Saint Sabbas (439–532), one of the most significant fathers of Palestinian monasticism, establishes his laura at Mar Saba, south of Jerusalem.

ca. 500

Saint Caesarius, monk-bishop of Arles, writes his *Regula ad monachos* for men. Thirty-four years later he writes a *Regula ad virgines* for consecrated women.

549

The death of Saint Finnian, "the teacher of all Ireland in his day," who founded Cleonard, one of the first great Irish monasteries. He drew his monastic inspiration from his visits to Welsh monasteries. Finnian's disciples included such saints and monastic founders as Saint Columba of Iona, Saint Brendan, Saint Kieran of Clonmacnois, and Saint Kenneth of Derry.

ca. 565

Saint Columba (521–597), coming from Ireland, establishes a monastery on the island of Iona, where even today a Protestant community, drawing inspiration from the monastic heritage, continues to flourish.

590

A monk who was to become known in the West as Saint Gregory the Great (†604) is elected pope. He wrote five books of dialogues for the edification of his people, the second of which gives us the life story of Saint Benedict of Nursia.

ca. 591

Saint Columbanus (543–615) sets out from Ireland to bring the Irish monastic heritage to France by establishing Luxeuil, and then to Italy, founding Bobbio in 615.

596

Pope Saint Gregory sends Saint Augustine and forty monks to England, where they establish a monastery at Canterbury.

ca. 600

Saint Catherine's monastery, built at the foot of Mount Sinai by Justinian, becomes the most vital center of Eastern Christian monasticism. The *Ladder of Paradise* of Saint John Climacus, monk of Sinai, synthesizes the ascetic and mystical tradition of the East.

628

Pope Honorius I for the first time exempts a monastery, Bobbio, from episcopal jurisdiction and places it immediately under papal care, thus acknowledging the monks' mission to the whole Church rather than to a particular diocese.

657

Saint Hilda (†680), who was baptized in 627 with Edwin, the ruler of Northumbria, establishes a monastery at Whitby for both nuns and monks. Such double monasteries, apart from Gilbert of Simpringham's twelfth-century revival, are rare outside of Anglo-Saxon times.

685

Saint Bede, later called the Venerable (672–735), enters Jarrow and begins fifty years of monastic life filled with *ora et labora*. His phenomenal scholarship produced the *Monumental Ecclesiastical History of the English People, History of the Abbots, Life of Cuthbert,* three books on the Apocalypse of Saint John, and many other significant works.

709

Saint Theodore establishes a strict cenobitic reform based on the writings of Saint Basil the Great and on Palestinian monasticism in the Studion monastery in Constantinople.

716

Saint Boniface (ca. 672–753) arrives in the Rhineland to begin the work that would make him the great organizer of German Christianity, building on the work of Saint Wilfrid, Saint Willibrord, and other monks. He founded the famed abbey of Fulda in 746.

816–818

Three meetings of abbots at Aachen under the leadership of Saint Benedict of Aniane (†821) sought to implement Charlemagne's decree that all monks observe the *Rule* of Saint Benedict of Nursia and uniform customs. To this end Benedict prepared a *Codex Regularum* or collection of Eastern and Western rules, and a *Concordia regularum,* a commentary on the *Rule,* seeking to show by comparison its unique superiority.

909

The foundation of Cluny by William of Aquitaine. In the course of the next two centuries Cluny would enjoy the rule of four outstanding abbots –Majolus (948–994), Odilo (994–1049), Hugh (1049–1109), and Peter the Venerable (1122–1157)—who would exercise immediate jurisdiction over some 2,000 monasteries.

ca. 970

King Edgar (†975) promulgates the *Regularis Concordia* drawn up by Saint Ethlwald (†984) with the consent of Saint Dunstan (909–988) in an effort to establish a uniform and fervent observance in English monasteries.

ca. 1000

The founding of Fonte Avellana by Ludulf (†1047), a disciple of Saint Romuald. It flourished under Saint Peter Damian (†1072) and became known for writings on asceticism, liturgy, and canon law, as well as for its role in the Gregorian reform, when it became the head of an eremitical congregation.

ca. 1012

Saint Romuald of Revenna (ca. 950–1027) establishes a cenobitical monastery on land granted him by Count Maldoli and, two miles higher, in the midst of a forest, an eremitical colony out of which developed the Camaldolese Congregation of monk-hermits.

1022

Saint Symeon the New Theologian dies after initiating a reform based on the tradition of the Desert Fathers, stressing the importance of the cell, silence, and reading as dispositions to develop pure prayer.

1073

The death of Saint John Gualbert (b.ca. 990), founder of Vallombroso, a reform based on a strict interpretation of the *Rule* of Saint Benedict, anticipating the reforms of Tiron, Savigny, and

Citeaux. Vallombroso also introduced into the hitherto homogenous monastic community a class of nonclerical *conversi* which evolved into the lay brothers, so successful at early Citeaux.

1084

Saint Bruno (ca. 1030–1101), with six companions, establishes the Grande Chartreuse about thirty miles from Grenoble out of which evolved the Carthusian order. The fifth prior, Guigo (1109–1136), compiled their *Consuetudines* (customs) in 1127; these, supplemented by ordinances of the general chapters, have guided the life of the monk-hermits and lay brothers and the expansion of the order till there were 195 charterhouses in 1521. Nuns have been affiliated to the order since the twelfth century. The only Carthusian house in the Western hemisphere is at Arlington, Vermont.

1098

On the feast of Saint Benedict, Palm Sunday, Saint Robert of Molesmes (†1112), his prior Alberic (†1109), subprior Stephen Harding (†1136), and eighteen others establish the New Monastery later called Citeaux.

1115

Saint Bernard of Fontaines, who entered Citeaux three years earlier with thirty relatives and friends, is sent to establish Clairvaux. Before his death in 1153 Clairvaux would found or adopt over 160 monasteries while the abbot would form a school of mystical spirituality and serve ecclesial and civil leaders as an effective arbiter.

1119

Pope Callistus II approves the *Charter of Charity,* which established the Cistercian order and brought to monastic life a new form of federated government with autonomous monasteries joined in general chapter providing a visitation system.

ca. 1120

The foundation of Tart, near Dijon, the first convent of nuns to adopt the Cistercian observance.

1216

The Lateran Council, inspired by the relatively good experience of the Cistercians, requires all monasteries to band together in provincial chapters and establish systems of visitation.

1344

Saint Sergius (1314–1392), a key figure in the great expansion of cenobitic monasticism in fourteenth-century Russia, establishes his first monastery in the north. In 1354 at the request of the Patriach of Constantinople he founded Holy Trinity Larva.

The Sienese Bernard Tolomes establishes a reformed monastery devoted to penance and poverty on Monte Oliveto, from which sprung the Olivetan congregation.

1408

Pope Gregory XII appoints the Venetian Ludovicus Barba (1318–1443) abbot of Santa Giustina of Padua, where he fostered a reform that became the nucleus of a congregation. As the congregation evolved supreme authority was placed in the hands of an annual general chapter (with an abbot and delegate from each house). This congregation form of federation was imitated with modifications by Monte Cassino, Vallodolid, Saint Vannes, Saint Maur, and the reformed congregation of Subiaco (in the mid-nineteenth century).

1515

Josif Volotsky, author of the *Short and Long Rules* (the last Russian monastic rules to be written), dies (ca. 1440). He represented a more institutional monasticism comparable to Cluny in spirit that opposed the more pneumatic and simple monastic life fostered by Saint Nil Sorsky (1433–1508).

1523

The reform initiated among the Camaldolese by Paolo Giustiniani (1476–1528) brings about the establishment of the autonomous congregation of Monte Corona.

1536

The English Parliament suppresses 243 smaller abbeys and priories. By 1539 the rest of the monasteries of the realm became forfeit to the Crown. Abbots and monks were put to death for refusing to accept Henry VIII as head of the Church.

1581

The Benedictine monastery of Bahia (Brazil) is founded, inaugurating monastic life in Latin America.

1604

Through the zealous efforts of Dom Didier de la Cour (1550–1632), the Congregation of Saint Vannes is established. It rapidly embraced a dozen neighboring monasteries and ultimately comprised some fifty houses. Great emphasis was laid on monastic training; study and literary occupation were seen as the normal "work" for a monk.

1618

A new congregation of Saint Maur is formed of monasteries around Paris. It developed into a flourishing, fervent, and erudite group that gave birth to one of the golden epochs (1650–1720) of Benedictine history.

1664

Abbot Armand de Rancé of La Trappe (1626–1670) adopted a rigorous interpretation of the Cistercian ideal, influenced by the Fathers of the Desert. This reform would give its name and inspiration to the Cistercians of the Strict Observance until the renewal after the Second Vatican Council.

1789

On the eve of the French revolution more than half the monasteries surviving in Europe were ruled by commendatory, absent, or even secular abbots and the number of monks and nuns had greatly declined. Twenty-five years later only twenty percent of these monasteries were still inhabited by monastics; many were completely destroyed.

1825

After an abortive attempt in New York, the first permanent monastic community in North America is established by the Cistercians (Trappists) at Tracadie in Nova Scotia. This community later transferred to the United States, becoming Saint Joseph's Abbey, Spencer, Massachusetts.

1833

Dom Prosper Guéranger (1805–1875) re-establishes Benedictine life at the priory of Solesmes. It became the center of a new congregation and began to exercise widespread influence through its liturgical work. The expulsion of the monks of Solesmes from France in 1880, 1882, and 1901 led to the founding of monasteries in England, Spain, Luxembourg, and Holland. Guéranger also supported the establishment of the Benedictine nuns at Sainte Cécile.

1850

Pope Pius IX names Pietro Casaretto (1810–1878) abbot of Subiaco in view of a reform of the Cassinese Congregation. Casaretto aggregated monasteries in many countries until in 1872 a new congregation of the Primitive Observance was established.

1852

Pope Pius IX re-establishes the Cassinese Benedictine congregation in Italy.

1854

Saint Meinrad's monastery is founded in Indiana to be a refuge for the monks of Einsiedeln. With Conception Abbey, founded in 1872, it formed the Swiss-American Congregation in 1881.

1855

Saint Vincent's monastery in Latrobe, Pennsylvania, founded by Dom Boniface Wimmer (†1887), who arrived in Pittsburgh in 1846, is raised to the dignity of an abbey to become the source of the American Cassinese Congregation.

1865

The Reverend R. M. Benson and Charles Ward establish the Society of Saint John the Evangelist (Cawley Fathers), the oldest existing monastic order in the Anglican Church, on the outskirts of Oxford.

1868

The Wolter brothers, disciples of Dom Guéranger and founders of Beuron (1862), receive papal approval to establish the Beuronese Congregation on the same lines as Solesmes' French congregation. Beuron would channel Guéranger's ideas and priorities to its offshoots—the Belgium, Brazilian, and Saint Ottilien Congregations—and to the Benedictine order at large, through the international Benedictine College of Sant 'Anselmo at Rome.

1883

The Cistercians (Trappists) establish the first Christian monastic community in China: Our Lady of Consolation, near Peking. This community was dispersed by the communists after the Second World War. Many of the monks were martyred, while the rest continue to live in fidelity to their monastic commitment as best they can among their families and friends.

1884

The Congregation of Saint Ottilien is founded as a missionary outreach in the spirit of Saint Boniface. It has abbeys or priories in Korea, Manchuria, East Africa (two abbeys with over two hundred monks in each), Zululand, Venezuela, and the United States.

1892

The Cistercians are divided into two orders. The Strict Observance (Trappists) today include some ninety monasteries of monks and fifty-five of nuns in all parts of the world. The rest of the Cistercians, divided into fourteen congregations, are united under a general chapter.

1893

In the Apostolic Brief, *Summum semper,* Pope Leo XIII tries to bring the various congregations of the monastic family together into a more unified order.

1923

Dom Columba Marmion (b. 1858), one of the most widely read monastic writers of the first half of the twentieth century, dies at Maredsous. His cause for canonization has been introduced at Rome.

1926

Dom Denys Prideux moves his community to Nashdom, where they become the first solidly established Benedictine community in the Anglican Church.

1950

The foundation of Shantivanam, a Benedictine ashram on the banks of the Kavery near Kalitalai, Tamil Nadu, South India, where Father Jules Monchanin and Father Henri Le Saux, O.S.B., seek to adapt Benedictine monasticism to Indian culture. In 1956 another ashram taking its inspiration from the *Rule* of Saint Benedict, this time following the interpretation of the Cistercians (Trappists), was founded at Kurisumala in Kerala by Father Francis Acharya, O.C.S.O.

1952

Pope Pius XII approves the *Lex propria* for the Confederation of Monastic Congregations of the Order of Saint Benedict. The Confederation has an Abbot Primate elected for twelve years. All the abbots meet in a congress each six years.

1958

The first community of Camaldolese monk-hermits is established in America at Big Sur, California. The Monte Corona Congregation established a hermitage at McConnelsville, Ohio, the next year.

1968

In the midst of the first Pan-Asian Monastic Conference at Bangkok, Thomas Merton (Father M. Louis of Gethsemani) is accidentally electrocuted. His extensive writings, translated into many languages, made not only the Catholic community, but even secular society, more aware of the existence, meaning, and mission of Western Christian monasticism.

For Further Reading

Sources

To get in touch with the spirit that animates monastic life you will want to go to those sources that give expression to the experiences that shaped the tradition in its beginnings and during the golden age of monasticism in the Middle Ages. Thanks to Cistercian Publications (Kalamazoo, Michigan 49008), many of these are now readily available in English in the Cistercian Studies Series (CS): *The Sayings of the Desert Fathers* (CS 59, 1975), translated by Benedicta Ward, S.L.G., who also introduces Norman Russell's translation of *The Lives of the Desert Fathers* (CS 34, 1981); the impressive three-volume *Pachomian Koimonia* (CS 45–47, 1980–82), by Armand Veilleux, O.C.S.O., which includes the lives, rules, and other writings of Saint Pachomius and his disciples; Evagrius Ponticus' *Praktikos and Chapters on Prayer* (CS 4, 1970, introduced and translated by John Eudes Bomberger, O.C.S.O.); Gregory of Nyssa's *Life of Moses* (CS 31, 1978), introduced and translated by Abraham J. Malherbe and Everett Ferguson, which gives a fundamental insight into the spirit of primitive monasticism in Cappadocia; and the *Discourses and Sayings* of Dorotheos of Gaza (CS 33, 1977), translated by Eric P. Wheeler, a text commonly given to eastern monastic novices to introduce them to the Syrian cenobitic tradition. Saint Athanasius' *Life of Anthony,* translated by Robert T. Meyer, has been published in the Ancient Christian Writers series (vol. 10, 1950).

Some of the *Conferences* of Saint John Cassian can be found in *Western Asceticism,* translated by Owen Chadwick (Philadelphia: Westminster, 1958); all of them, in the Nicene and Post-Nicene Fathers series, vol. 11, translated by Edgar C. S. Gibson (Grand Rapids: Eerdmans, 1955).

The *Long and Short Rules* of Saint Basil can be found among his ascetical works published by the Catholic University of America in their Fathers of the Church series (vol. 9, 1950), translated by M. Monica Wagner, C.S.C.). Cistercian Publications has also given us Luke Eberle, O.S.B.'s translation of *The Rule of the Master* (CS 6, 1977).

In commemoration of the fifteen-hundredth anniversary of the birth date traditionally ascribed to Saint Benedict of Nursia, A.D. 480, the American Benedictines produced *RB 1980*

(Collegeville, MN: The Liturgical Press, 1980), containing a translation of his *Rule for Monasteries,* a very extensive introduction, notes, a two-hundred page appendix with longer expositions of monastic topics, a Latin concordance, and various indexes—a very good and useful tool.

The second book of Pope Saint Gregory the Great's *Dialogues*—"The Life and Miracles of Saint Benedict" (translated by Alexius Hoffmann, O.S.B.—was also published by Collegeville (1925), as was Carmela Viscello Franklin's *Early Monastic Rules* (1982). The University of Notre Dame Press published *The Ancrene Rule: A Rule for Religious Women* (translated by M. B. Salu) in 1956. In 1951 Oxford University Press, New York, published *Monastic Constitutions of Lonfranc,* by David Knowles, O.S.B.

The Cistercian Fathers Series (Cistercian Publications), which already contains over forty volumes and is still in full production, makes available almost all the significant writings of the great Cistercian Fathers of the golden age.

In the Cistercian Studies series classics of other traditions are represented, such as: *The Ladder of Monks and Twelve Meditations* of Gurgo II, ninth prior of the Grande Chartreuse (CS 48, 1981), translated by Edmund Colledge, O.S.A., and Father James Walsh, S.J., and *The Practical and Theological Chapters* and *The Three Theological Discourses* of Saint Symeon the New Theologian (CS 41, 1982), translated by Paul McGuckin, C.P.

Studies of Spirituality

Besides the excellent introductions to be found with the foregoing translations of the sources, there are many good studies or presentations of the spirituality they present. Irénée Hausherr, S.J., reaches into the very heart of Eastern monastic spirituality with his two studies, both from Cistercian Publications: *Penthos: The Doctrine of Compunction in the Christian East* (CS 53, 1982) and *The Name of Jesus* (CS 44, 1978). Louis Bouyer brings his usual insight and clarity to his study of *The Meaning of the Monastic Life* (New York: Kenedy, 1955). The studies in *The Continuing Quest for God: Monastic Spirituality in Tradition and Transition,* edited by William Skudlarek, O.S.B. (Collegeville, 1982), give a sweeping overview of twenty centuries. Jean Leclercq's *Alone with God* (New York: Farrar, Strauss and Cudahy, 1961) is a study of the spirituality of eremitical monastic life.

116

Modern Presentations of Monastic Spirituality

If *The Principles of Monasticism,* by Maurus Wolter, O.S.B. (Saint Louis: Herder, 1962), might be seen as representative of the Benedictine spirituality of the nineteenth-century revival, *Vision of Peace,* by Wilfrid Tunink, O.S.B. (New York: Farrar Straus, 1963), represents the twentieth century before the Second Vatican Council. Modern Cistercian monastic spirituality is well presented by Thomas Merton (Father M. Louis, O.C.S.O.) in *The Monastic Journey,* edited by Patrick Hart (Mission, KS: Sheed, Andrews and McMeil, 1977), and other works. Some of the contemporary struggle to bring traditional monastic spirituality into our times is revealed in symposia: *The Cistercian Spirit: A Symposium in Memory of Thomas Merton* (CS 3, 1969), *Rule and Life: An Interdisciplinary Symposium* (CS 12, 1971), and *Contemplative Community* (CS 21, 1972), all edited by M. Basil Pennington, O.C.S.O., for Cistercian Publications.

A candid picture of present-day monastic life and spirituality may be found in some of the journals, such as *The Sign of Jonas,* by Merton (New York: Harcourt, Brace, 1953), *Jubilee: A Monk's Journal,* by M. Basil Pennington, O.C.S.O. (New York: Paulist, 1981), and *Genesee Diary* by Henri Nouwen (New York: Doubleday, 1976). The most delightful presentation of monastic spirituality ever published is the penetrating cartoon book *The Life of Little Saint Placid* by Genevieve Gallois, O.S.B. (New York: Pantheon, 1956).

An excellent study of modern Eastern Christian monastic spirituality is that of Russian Archbishop Ignatius Briachaninov, *The Arena: An Offering to Contemporary Monasticism* (Madras: Diocesan Press, 1970). A good comparative study of Eastern and Western monastic spirituality yesterday and today is *One yet Two: Monastic Tradition East and West* (CS 29, 1976), edited by M. Basil Pennington, O.C.S.O., for Cistercian Publications. A candid view of contemporary Eastern monastic spirituality as it is lived at the heart of Orthodoxy is found in Pennington's *O Holy Mountain: Journal of a Retreat on Mount Athos* (New York: Doubleday, 1978).

Monastic Culture

Monks have a culture as well as a spirituality; the one shapes the other, and both are influenced profoundly by the times. Jean Leclercq, O.S.B., has been the foremost scholar in this domain, as in most areas of monastic studies in our times. *The Love of Learning and the Desire for*

God: A Study of Monastic Culture (New York: Fordham, 1961) is now considered a classic. His more particular studies include such fascinating studies as *Monks on Marriage: A Twelfth-Century View* (New York: Seabury, 1982) and *Monks and Love in Twelfth Century France* (Oxford: Clarendon, 1979). Desmond Seward's *Monks and Wine* (New York: Crown, 1979) is also interesting.

Monastic History

Obviously, it is not possible to separate completely studies of spirituality and culture and history when we are considering an historical phenomenon, but there are studies that are primarily historical in their considerations.

David Knowles, O.S.B., gives us probably the best concise survey in *Christian Monasticism* (New York: McGraw-Hill, 1961). Early monastic history is studied by Jacques Lacarriere, *Men Possessed by God: The Story of the Desert Monks of Ancient Christendom* (New York: Doubleday, 1964), and Derwas J. Chitty, *The Desert a City: An Introduction to the Study of Egyptian and Palestinian Monasticism under the Christian Empire* (Oxford: Blackwell, 1966.)

There are some interesting studies of monastic life in different centuries: H. E. J. Cowdrey, *The Cluniacs and the Gregorian Reform* (Oxford: Clarendon, 1970); Bede Lockner, O.CIST., *Eleventh-Century Background of Citeaux* (CS 8, 1972, Cistercian Publications); and Bennett D. Hill, *English Cistercian Monasteries and Their Patrons in the Twelfth Century* (Urbana: University of Illinois, 1968). *Benedictine Monasticism: Its Foundations and Development Through the Twelfth Century,* by Lowrie J. Daly, S.J. (New York: Sheed and Ward, 1965) is complemented by Sacheverell Sitwell's *Monks, Nuns and Monasteries* (New York: Holt, Rinehart, and Winston, 1965), which moves from the Middle Ages to modern times. Louis Lekai, O.CIST., has recently published a very complete study of *The Cistercians: Ideals and Reality* (Kent State University, 1977), but his outlook needs to be modified in some cases by that of scholars from the Strict Observance.

Coleman J. Barry, O.S.B., brings Benedictine life to America in *Worship and Work* (Collegeville, 1956), and Thomas Merton chronicles American Cistercian life in *The Waters of Siloe* (New York: Harcourt, Brace, 1949).

There are no good studies of modern Eastern monasticism except those on Mount Athos, such as *Athos. Mountain of Light,* by Chrysostomos Dahm, O.S.B. (Ottenburg: Burda, 1959) and John Julius Norwich and Reresby Sitwell's *Mount Athos* (New York: Harper & Row, 1966).

Protestant Monasticism

One of the exciting developments in modern monasticism has been the recovery of monastic life by the churches that separated from Rome in the sixteenth century. The Anglicans were first in this, but it is Taizé that has received the most attention. Francois Beat did a general study, *The Rise of Protestant Monasticism* (Baltimore: Helicon, 1963). John Heijke studied Taizé from a Catholic viewpoint: *An Ecumenical Light on the Renewal of Religious Community Life: Taizé* (Pittsburgh: Duquesne, 1967). But to understand Taizé you need to study *The Rule of Taizé* (New York: Seabury, 1974).

India

Another exciting development is the implantation of an indigenous Christian monasticism in non-Western cultures, of which India is the leading example. Jules Monchanin and Henri Le Saux, O.S.B., the pioneers, recount their adventures in *A Benedictine Ashram* (Douglas, 1964). M. Basil Pennington, O.C.S.O., takes a candid look at where this is today in *Monastic Journey to India* (New York: Seabury, 1982).

The New American Monasticism

Monasticism is exerting a widespread influence and attraction today in the West, within and without the bounds of Christianity. An interesting survey of what is happening in America is *Living Together Alone: The New American Monasticism,* by Charles Fracchia (San Francisco: Harper & Row, 1978).

Lives

Monastic spirituality, culture, and history are fleshed out and best experienced in the concrete lives of monks and nuns. It was the *Lives of the Fathers of the Desert,* and above all Saint Athanasius' *Life of Anthony* and Sulpitius Severus' *Life of Saint Martin* (Nicene and Post-Nicene Fathers series, vol. 11, Grand Rapids: Eerdmans, 1955), that first spread this ideal widely in the Church. Pope Saint Gregory's *Dialogues* did much to popularize the Legislator of Monte Cassino. There are many good biographies that depict the monastic reality of the different ages. Owen Chadwick's *John Cassian* (Cambridge: University Press, 1968) bridges East and West. Peter Batselier's *Saint Benedict: Father of Western Civilization* (Antwerp: Mercatorfonds, 1980) describes Benedict and the history that proceeded from him; *Benedict's Disciples,* edited by D. H. Farmer (Leominster: Fowler Wright, 1980), fleshes out key monastics from fifteen centuries with an emphasis on the English: Cuthbert and Wilfrid, Hilda and Etheldreda, Bede and Boniface, Dunstan and Godric, Gertrude More, Ullathorne and Mary More. Central figures in Irish monasticism—Saints Brendan, Columba, and Columbanus—are brought alive in *The Quest of Three Abbots: Pioneers of Ireland's Golden Age,* by Brendan Lehave (London: J. Murray, 1968). The Cistercian Studies Series offers good biographies of the key Cistercian Fathers: Jean Leclercq, O.S.B., *Bernard of Clairvaux and the Cistercian Spirit* (CS 16, 1976); Aelred Squire, O.S.B., *Aelred of Rievaulx* (CS 50, 1981); and John-Marie Déchanet, O.S.B., *William of Saint Thierry: The Man and His Work* (CS 10, 1972).

Raymond Thibault, O.S.B., disciple of the greatest Benedictine of our times, has given us a real sense of his spiritual father in *Abbot Columba Marmion* (Saint Louis: Herder, 1949). Perhaps even better than a biography is *Thomas Merton, Monk: A Monastic Tribute,* edited by Patrick Hart, O.C.S.O. (Mission, KS: Andrews and McMeil, 1977), written by monks who lived with this great Cistercian and loved him. Elizabeth Isichei's *Entirely for God: The Life of Michael Iwene Tansi* (CS 43, 1980) is about the life of a Nigerian Cistercian who died in 1964; it examines the challenges involved in making Christian monastic life available to men and women of low-income nations (what some have called the Third World). *In Search of True Wisdom: Visits to Eastern Spiritual Fathers,* by Sergius Bolshokoff and M. Basil Pennington, O.C.S.O. (New York: Doubleday, 1979), presents the stories of Father Sergius of the Laura of Saint Alexander Nensky; Archimandrite Aimilianos, Hegumen of Simonos Petros; Mother Alexandra, Foundress of Holy Transfiguration Monastery; and a dozen other representatives of modern Eastern Christian monastic life.

Color Plate Captions

Jacket

Our Lady of Gethsemani, Kentucky. "The Lord is my shepherd, I shall not want; he makes me lie down in green pastures. He leads me beside still water; he restores my soul. He leads me in paths of righteousness for his name's sake" (Psalm 23:1–4).

1

Born in Nursia, Italy, in 480, Saint Benedict founded the Abbey of Montecassino and is considered to be the father of Western monastic orders. He drew up the code of monastic life—the *Rule* of Saint Benedict—whose famous motto is "ora et labora"—"pray and work." *Saint Benedict,* detail of a fifteenth-century fresco; Monte Oliveto Maggiore, Siena.

2

The bells mark the moments of the community's life; they ring out the first call in the morning and so on through the day until the final call to Compline.

3

Prie-dieu with rosary. The rosary is one of the older forms of contemplative Western prayer. While reciting the sequence of 150 Hail Marys, one is meant to concentrate on the fifteen episodes of the life of Jesus Christ that are called the "mysteries." The use of small beads made of stone, wood, or other materials to mark out prayers comes to us from the East. The name *rosary* seems to derive from the crowns of roses worn by the first martyrs. As the petals were stripped one by one from the crowns by the survivors, prayers were said.

4

The prayers contained in the breviary, which the Catholic Church encourages both religious and lay persons to use, have their origin in the Liturgy of the Hours. Monks or nuns are brought together in the early morning and several times during the day: Lauds, Terce, Sext, None, Vespers, and Compline.

5

Monastery of Saint Francis, Fiesole, Italy. A son of Saint Francis seen in the intimacy of a cloister.

6–7

The Abbey of Monte Oliveto Maggiore near Siena was begun in 1320. It is a majestic monastic complex, famed for its history and collection of art. Today it is a center for the restoration and rebinding of important texts and documents.

A *monastery* is a religious community or a place where a group of monks or nuns live together in austere simplicity and solitude. An *abbey* is a monastery with its own church and property to administer. It is always headed by an abbot or abbess who directs its life. A *convent* is a "generic" word for a place where a group of friars or sisters live together. A *hermitage* is a refuge, away from the world, where a dedicated man or woman seeks to live in solitude and in the contemplation of God.

8

A novice of the Order of the Poor Clares at prayer. A novice is one who is preparing to make his or her first vows. The Order of the Poor Clares was founded by Saint Francis for Saint Clare and her followers, who wished to emulate the Franciscan ideals of spirituality. Unlike the Franciscan male orders (Friars Minor, Conventuals, and Capuchins), the Poor Clares live a monastic life within an enclosure.

PRAYER

17

The clothing of a monk is the ceremony in which the monk becomes a member of the community that he has chosen and that has accepted him. *Life of the Blessed Umilta',* lateral panel; Uffizi Gallery, Florence; Pietro Lorenzetti (1280–1348).

18

New Camaldoli Hermitage, Big Sur, California. A monk in his cell.

19

La Grande Chartreuse, France. This monastery was built in 1084 by Hugues, Bishop of Grenoble. Legend says that the Bishop saw seven stars in his dream announcing the arrival of seven travelers in search of a retreat. They were led by Saint Bruno, for whom the Bishop built the monastery.

20

Our Lady of Gethsemani, Kentucky. Morning prayers. "My voice you shall hear in the morning, O Lord; in the morning will I direct my prayer to you, and will look up" (Psalm 5:3).

21

The Certosa (formerly a Carthusian monastery), Florence, Italy. A monk during solitary prayer. "But you, when you pray, enter into your room, and when you have shut the door, pray to your Father in secret. . . ." (Matthew 6:6).

22

Saint Joseph's Abbey, Spencer, Massachusetts. Burial of a monk. Photo by Brother Matthew Joseph; St. Joseph's Abbey.

23

New Camaldoli Hermitage, Big Sur, California. The cell is "a heaven" where the monastic retires to find solitude to establish his personal relationship with God through prayer, study, and rest.

24

Russian Orthodox Monastery of New Skete, Cambridge, New York. A priest giving a deacon Holy Communion during the liturgy.

25

(a) Saint Joseph's Abbey, Spencer, Massachusetts. Inaugurating the celebration of the Pascal Mystery with a procession through the cloister on Palm Sunday. (b) Saint Joseph's Abbey, Spencer, Massachusetts. The Abbot blessing the monks at the conclusion of the Easter Vespers. Photos by Brother Matthew Joseph; St. Joseph's Abbey.

26

La Verna, Italy. Following the monastic tradition of pilgrimage to the shrine of their saints, each day the friars and faithful make a procession to the cell of Saint Francis. Saint Francis often retired to this mountain retreat given to him in 1213. He died there on September 14, 1224.

27

New Clairveaux, Vina, California. Trappist monks celebrating a special benediction in honor of the Virgin Mary on December 8, feast of the Immaculate Conception.

28

Poor Clares in Montefalco, Italy. Nuns at prayer. The timeless tradition of The Hours has been a favorite subject in art.

WORK

37

Painting showing nuns at work. *Life of the Blessed Umilta'*, lateral panel; Uffizi Gallery, Florence; Pietro Lorenzetti (1280–1348).

38–39

Bavarian nuns bringing in the harvest. "Neither did we eat any man's bread for nought; but wrought with labor and travail night and day, that we might not be chargeable to any of you" (II Thessalonians 3:8).

40

Abbey of Monte Oliveto, Italy. A monk at the press cutting paper. Restoration and binding of manuscripts is an activity found in many monasteries. It is only thanks to this centuries-old tradition that many ancient texts have been preserved and have survived until today.

41

Illuminated manuscript showing nuns spinning wool. *Codice delle Suore,* detail of the month of January; Biblioteca Comunale, Siena; Sano di Pietro (1406–1481).

42

New Skete, Cambridge, New York. A monk painting a fresco in the monastery's new church.

43

(a) Monastery of Christ in the Desert, Abiquiu, New Mexico. Monks working at the loom. (b) New Clairveaux, Vina, California. A monk at his studies.

44

Star Cross Monastery, Annapolis, California. Farming is the principal activity in this community.

45

Saint Makarios, Coptic Monastery, Egypt. Coptic brothers working in the fields. Monks here, following the earliest Christian monastic traditions, have made a primary contribution to the greening of Egypt's desert, producing a large variety of vegetables and animal fodder.

46–47

In the second century, Saint Anthony the Anchorite retired into a desert region near Thebes, called Thebaid, establishing the kind of life depicted in this painting with its many various facets: solitary and communal prayer, hospitality, instruction, work in the gardens, care of the sick, burial of the dead, fishing in the river. The name Thebaid has come to mean a deserted place or a place of great peace and silence. *Thebaid*; Uffizi Gallery, Florence; G. Starnina (1354–1413).

48

Saint Makarios, Coptic Monastery, Egypt. A monk in the bindery of the monastery printing plant. These monks publish a variety of books and pamphlets on subjects from agriculture to catechism.

49

Fresco of Saint Benedict and the monks building the abbey of Monte Oliveto Maggiore. "Come to the Lord, the living stone rejected by man as worthless but chosen by God as valuable. Come as living stones, and let yourself be used in building the spiritual temple, where you will serve as holy priests to offer spiritual and acceptable sacrifices to God through Jesus Christ" (I Peter 2:4–5). *From the Life of Saint Benedict,* fresco; Monte Oliveto Maggiore, Siena; Sodoma (1477–1549).

50

San Galgano, Italy. A sister of the Olivetan order who has devoted sixty years of her life to painting icons.

51

Monastery of Christ in the Desert, Abiquiu, New Mexico. A monk in the pottery; ceramics contribute to the support of this monastery.

52

Nuns doing fine embroidery. The ancient virtues of patience and perfection are seen here as a practical occupation, but as in all works of the members of the religious orders, they stand for a way of life that calls for these virtues in all doings.

COMMUNITY

77

Saint Benedict distributing food to the monks in the refectory. Meals are important as serene and vital moments in the religious community. "Give us today our daily bread" (Matthew 6:11). *From the Life of Saint Benedict,* fresco; Monte Oliveto Maggiore, Siena; Sodoma (1477–1549).

78

Star Cross Monastery, Annapolis, California. A nun ringing the bell at dawn.

79

Hermitage of Camaldoli, Italy. Each monk enjoys a solitary cell within the community.

80

Benedictine Abbey, Melk, Austria. A view of the enormous complex of the Benedictine Abbey, built in 1702 by Abbot Dietmayr, on the River Danube. Its renowned library contains a collection of 80,000 books and 2,000 manuscripts. Photo by Heinz Müller-Brunke, Bernau/Obb; courtesy the Austrian National Tourist Office, New York.

81

The Blessed Umilta' reading to the nuns in the refectory. Silence is observed in many monasteries during meal times while a sister or brother reads from spiritual excerpts taken from the writing of the Fathers of the Church. "Go your way, eat your bread with joy, and drink your wine with a merry heart . . ." (Ecclesiastes 9:7). *Life of the Blessed Umilta',* lateral panel; Uffizi Gallery, Florence; Pietro Lorenzetti (1280–1348).

82

(a) Illuminated manuscript showing a monk playing a musical instrument. *Codex Squarchialupi;* Biblioteca Laurenziana, Florence. (b) A nun playing the organ. "Praise him with the sound of the trumpet, praise him with the psaltery and harp. Praise him with timbrel and dance: praise him with stringed instruments and organs" (Psalm 150:3–4).

83

New Clairveaux, Vina, California. Three members of the community reading at sunset.

84

The Carmine Altarpiece, detail side panel, stories of the Carmelite order. Siena Pienacoteca; Pietro Lorenzetti (1280–1348).

85

Anglican Benedictine Abbey, Nashdom, Berkshire, England. Monks walking in the garden.

86–87

Sisters in moments of recreation and joy.

88

St. Michael de Cuxa, Prades, France. Benedictine monastery from the twelfth century. The partial remains of one of the cloisters were bought and transported to the United States in 1925 and have been reconstructed within The Cloisters in New York.

97

Painting of Saint Catherine of Siena. One of the few religious women to come to prominence in the Middle Ages, Saint Catherine was born in Siena in 1347. She devoted herself to the poor and to the sick as well as taking part in public life. She went to Avignon where her decisive influence induced Pope Gregory XI to return to Rome. She was the center of spiritual revival everywhere she went. Though she never learned to write, she dictated hundreds of letters to the great of the day, as well as a notable mystic work called *The Dialogue of Saint Catherine of Siena.* Basilica of San Domenico, Siena; Andrea Vanni.

98

Chapel in the Monastery of Christ in the Desert, Abiquiu, New Mexico.

99

The Monastery of Christ in the Desert, Abiquiu, New Mexico. Built within the last twenty years, it emphasizes the importance of the church through its traditional monastic architectural style. As in old monasteries, the church is the largest building, dominating life both physically and spiritually.

100

New Skete, Cambridge, New York. Cupolas and crosses from the church.

101

The Certosa, Florence, Italy. A well in the center of the cloister is a constant architectural motif. A reminder of the days when water could only be supplied this way, it still has rich symbolic significance.

102

A hermit walking in the Egyptian desert. The desert is reality, in its essence; unencumbered by anything else: it is a place or a state of the soul where one can live alone with God.

103

The Tau, an ancient Hebrew symbol adopted by the nascent Christian faith. "Hurt not the earth, neither the sea nor the trees, till we have sealed the servants of our God in their foreheads" (Revelation 7:3).

104

Painting of Saint Bernardine of Siena preaching. Saint Bernardine (1380 1444) belonged to the Observant Congregation. He was one of the most effective and most widely known preachers of his day, and his popular and lively sermons are still read. The later mendicant friars brought the fruits of the monastic life into the streets and the squares of the cities to share them with the people. *Sermon of Saint Bernardino in Front of the Church of Saint Francis in Siena*; Chapter House, Siena; Sano di Pietro (1406–81).